BAM
BOLD ACHIEVEMENT METHOD

Accelerate Learning and Live a Richer Life

BRONKAR LEE & CYNDI HARVELL LEE

Visit www.bamthebook.com

This title is available at special discounts for bulk purchases in the United States by corporations, institutions, and other organizations. For more information, please contact info@bamthebook.com.

ISBN: 978-1537394084

Second Edition

Cover design by Anurup Ghosh
Interior artwork/photos from Cyndi Harvell Lee, Le Anima, Shutterstock
Edited by William Barr

BOOK EXTRAS

- Bold Achievement Manual (a workbook of action steps, questions and guidance to go with each chapter)
- Bonus videos
- Audio meditation tune-ups
- Resource lists
- Worksheets

Available for free at bamthebook.com/extras

DEDICATION

For hellos and goodbyes, beginnings and endings, inhales and exhales.

For our son Elijah and Grandma Bronkar—two authentic souls who have shown us the power of pure laughter and joy.

CONTENTS

Bronkar, Cyndi & Elijah - June 2016

"Life is either a daring adventure or nothing."

—Helen Keller

WHO IS THIS GUY AND WHY SHOULD I LISTEN TO HIM?

My name is Bronkar. Yes, that's my real name (my mom's maiden name, in fact), and no, I'm not a Viking. I'm a coach, speaker, author, and entertainer. I started my career as a street musician drumming on buckets at the corner of East Clayton and College Avenue in my hometown of Athens, Georgia. In my early 20s, I facilitated drum therapy sessions and self-expression workshops for kids and young adults before moving to San Francisco to attend clown school (true story!). Upon graduating, I toured Switzerland as the ringmaster of a circus and later created my one-man show (incorporating the art form of beatbox juggling), while putting in some time as a personal trainer. Inspirational entertainment and speaking became my full-time career. My wife, Cyndi, and I moved to Los Angeles, and I traveled around the world performing for festivals, conferences, TV shows, theaters and cruise ships. We then moved our home base to Atlanta, reconnecting with our roots, so we could start our family and I could continue my growth as a speaker.

But let's back up a couple decades before all this ex-

Bronkar as ringmaster in Switzerland's Circus Monti - 2006

citing stuff happened, to a time when I was an elementary school kid with an excessive amount of energy and was diagnosed with severe ADHD. Most of my teachers put me in a box and labeled it: "Talks too much / Moves too much / Acts too much." I was lonely, lost, and never felt like I fit in. Teachers told me repeatedly that I needed to sit still, calm down, and be quiet. The belief that this was the only way to learn and I just wasn't good at it was instilled in my brain. The distracted kid with too much energy became the angry, confused, explosive teenager. At 270 pounds, I was a bullet train of a dude, falling face first into every bad situation possible and throwing emotional bombs at all my relationships. I didn't know where to direct my energy, so I plugged it into getting wasted, eating excessively, and making questionable

Bronkar, 18, graduating high school

life choices. My parents kicked me out of the house more than once. I totaled two cars and should've died several times. I basically overdid EVERYTHING in all the wrong ways.

It wasn't until I got to my early 20s that I realized there was another option. The people who made me feel small and stupid were wrong about me! I *could* learn, and I could do it well, if I just created my own rules. So I rewrote the system. Success came when I did it my way, when I turned it into an adventure and an experience I could be excited to engage in. From that moment on, life changed for the better.

The challenges that I faced early on in my life pushed me to those discoveries. The years of turbulence and disorder allowed me to shape my own system of learning that led me to places I never would have imagined. I'm still that crazy, overly enthusiastic and spirited ten-year-old, and yes, part of me is still that wild and vulnerable teenager. But I've learned how to channel it and where to channel it so that I get positive results. And if I can create success from madness, then anyone can.

Bronkar, 34, beatbox juggling

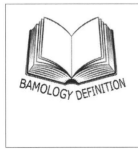

sanity goddess
/**san**-i-tee **god**-is/

noun
A seemingly otherworldly being who exudes peace and radiates a calming energy. The perfect partner for a crazy, unorganized, ADHD human being.

Part of the reason I was able to even out and gain focus is because of my wife and sanity goddess, Cyndi. She's my polar opposite. Where I'm extreme, she's grounded. Where I'm hyper, she's mellow. Where I'm scatterbrained, she's centered. An English minor, prolific songwriter, and creative mastermind, Cyndi used her word magic and organizational skills to help me put my method into book form so that it would make sense to outside eyes.

Above all, Cyndi and I share some basic values and philosophies that made us obvious partners for the book. (And for life!) We believe in being active participants in our lives. We believe we have the power to create our own story, and we believe that even when we're in situations that aren't optimal, we can still live as inspired, energized, and effective human beings. Happiness is a choice.

"Twenty years from now you will be more disappointed by the things that you didn't do than by the ones you did do, so throw off the bowlines, sail away from safe harbor, catch the trade winds in your sails. Explore, Dream, Discover."

– Mark Twain

INTRODUCTION

You're standing on a cliff's edge. Direct your eyes downward and your vision is obstructed by fog. You aren't able to see where the nothingness turns to earth again. Direct your eyes straight across the chasm and you see abundance— green trees that glow with life, lush with fruit and flowers, appealing to you because it's better than where you stand. Maybe where you are seems gray and empty. Or maybe it is just a little bit less luxurious than what's over there. Either way, over here is one thing, and over there is **better**.

Look to your right and you see a bridge leading to the greener side. It looks safe, but there's an adventurous charm to it, and it's definitely epic, like there should be extreme orchestral theme music as you cross it. It's a few feet from where you are now. And once you get to the bridge entrance, it's just a series of small steps to get to the better side. You don't have to jump across the void. You don't have to build your own bridge from scratch. You don't have to dive toward a swinging rope, backflip onto a floating trampoline, and catapult over shooting fireballs to get there. You just have to make a choice. Yes or no.

If you don't want to learn anything new, you don't want to achieve something, you're not interested in being inspired or ignited into taking action... then walking toward the bridge isn't for you. This book isn't for you. Put it down and get back to your regularly scheduled program. This book is for those of you eager for knowledge and ready to expand your mind. It's for those of you who know deep down that you have the potential to be better. No matter how amazing you are now. This book is for you. And a little bit for me. I have to remind myself of these things constantly. So this is for all of us.

It's about more than just going through the motions and practicing some techniques to hone a certain skill. If you'll allow it, it's also about finding your authentic self and being that person every day. It's about living with passion. Not just following a passion, but *being* passionate and then applying that energy to every aspect of your life. We're getting deep, guys. Hope you brought your scuba gear. Let's explore life below the surface.

Learning a new skill is a big deal, especially as we get older and have more and more responsibilities and time commitments. Adulting is hard, my friends. *Am I right?!* We are supposed to balance sleeping, eating, cleaning, working, exercising, caring, and relaxing, along with a whole other slew of "-ings." And let's be clear. Relaxing is a bonus that doesn't always make it onto the list. We work hard and we don't have a lot of time, so it can drive us crazy when we don't see progress as quickly as we'd like.

I totally get it. That's what inspired me to write this

book. You don't have to embark on the learning journey solo! And you don't have to create your own system from scratch. You don't have to make giant, unprecedented leaps, and you don't have to work miracles or invoke the supernatural. You take one small step at a time. It's like nachos. Put a party platter of cheesy, beany, salsa-and-sour-cream goodness in front of me, and I can devour the whole thing. But I do it chip by chip and chew by chew. (You didn't know that you would hear learning is like eating nachos, did you? You're welcome.)

The Bold Achievement Method is about fiercely stepping up to the plate and owning who you are in order to go after what you want. There's just not enough time in our lives to waste it on being hesitant, afraid, and indecisive. Expanding our minds and growing our abilities should be an adventure. It should light up our eyes, fill up our hearts, and lift up our spirits.

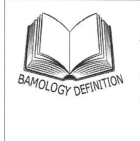

bold
/bohld/

adjective
Courageous, daring and imaginative; not hesitating to break the rules of the "norm"; how you will feel when you take actions on your goals

LEARNING IS LIMITLESS

What's the first thing you visualize in your mind when someone mentions the word learning? Is it a classroom? Well, whether you envision that or not, there's no denying that most of us spent a lot of years in one. Maybe you have wonderful memories of that time period. I hope you do. But there are some of us who had a less-than-ideal experience, and we are now faced with the challenge of breaking the negative association that we have with the word learning.

I was a kid with a lot of zest for life (to put it mildly), and reading books and sitting in a classroom turned me off from education. It didn't work for me. Things weren't taught in a way that I could grasp. So of course I was diagnosed with ADHD and told I needed drugs to "correct" it. Now, this isn't a book about pharmaceuticals or the public school system so we can pause that conversation for another time. But it is about the fact that I've learned an incredible amount of skills post-school and managed to do so with an insane amount of focus. It's because my process is all about **DOING**. I channelled my wild and unbridled energy into jumping in and taking action.

My wife, Cyndi, was the complete opposite of me when it came to school. She was into books and studying, and yet she was bored and never felt challenged enough. She was always waiting for someone to lead her to knowledge, and no one ever came. Maybe you are like she is. Or maybe you are like I am. Maybe you think learning is for kids. Maybe you think it ends once you finish college or high school, as though it's time to stop learning and time to "do life." Maybe you don't even realize you hold these beliefs.

My point is, let's scrap whatever negative associations we have with the word and make new positive ones. Learning is a part of all stages of life, whether you realize it or not. The more you are aware of it, the more you can absorb. Cyndi and I are learning how to be parents right now with our new son Elijah. We're getting a fresh perspective on life by watching how he learns and sees the world. We didn't have a baby because we wanted to go back to school. But here we are, learning! (And loving it, I might add.) I think it *feels* like it gets harder the older we get, but that's because we've had more time to develop excuses, and we've had more challenges that have instilled in us a fear of failing. They're all stories we've created in our heads, things we tell ourselves based on that fear.

I interviewed several people in various fields as I worked on this book—from school teacher to Olympic gymnast to Broadway performer—all people with unique and positive perspectives on learning, who value the process and its power. When asked what they thought of when they heard the word, some of the responses were: "Endless possibilities." "Limitless." "Achieving new things." "Expanding awareness." "Evolution." How's that for positive association?

The concept of neuroplasticity describes the brain as malleable. When you practice something over and over, it literally changes your brain! Your neural networks reshape themselves and create stronger pathways. YOU have control over this. Wow. There's no age limit. There's no prerequisite. There's just you. Making a decision to do. (I didn't even *intend* to rhyme. My poet brain pathways are on fire!) If you can refashion your perspective on learning to be one of open-hearted readiness, there are no limits to what you can accomplish.

CREATING YOUR CONCENTRATED AWESOMENESS

Learning a skill really boils down to two main components: time and energy. Yes, there are other pieces involved. But you won't get anywhere without investing time and energy. (*I wanted to just print those two words on a page and call it a day, but Cyndi said we needed more text to sell a book. Crazy Cyndi!*) The more you devote, the better you will be. It's pretty simple, even though we often make it more complicated in our own minds.

I modeled the Bold Achievement Method after my experiences with learning to play the saxophone. I had to put in the hours and make them count. But most importantly, I altered my perception of time, directing exceptionally focused attention into every minute of my practice, creating what I call **concentrated awesomeness.**

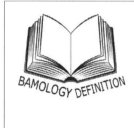

concentrated awesomeness
/**kon**-suh n-trey-tid **aw**-suh m nis/

noun
Maximum potency of greatness that results from channeling every ounce of your energy and focus into something

BAMOLOGY DEFINITION

Basically this means you get more value out of the time you have, whether that is 5 minutes or 60 minutes a day. Time and having enough of it is a big factor in many people's decisions to take on a new project. I want to make it clear that you *can* work a full-time job and have a family and mow your lawn and pay your bills...and still create the space to learn. (And those other aspects of your life that you're so busy with will be better for it.) But you must be fully committed to your goal, prepared to give it a fighting chance, and ready to squeeze as much concentrated awesomeness as you can out of the time you have. (What's that? You want a little poem to hit the point home?)

You focus your brain
You practice and train
Your goals and your dreams clearly stated

You get what you give
And love what you live
Your awesomeness so concentrated

CHOOSE YOUR OWN ADVENTURE

Our individual lives are just a long string of choices. You don't always have complete control over what happens, but you do have control over your responses. Years ago, I made a choice to drop everything and drive to California with Cyndi so that I could go to circus school. We sold all our stuff and camped our way across the country in a blue minivan with 200,000 miles on it. That choice prompted the opportunity to travel through Switzerland for a year as a ringmaster in a circus. This wasn't necessarily what I was looking for, but I said yes! It led me to more opportunities to create my own one-man show (which I said yes to), and that, in turn, led to even more opportunities. I kept saying yes. I kept getting opportunities. *Get it?*

A lot of us have ingrained beliefs about how the world

works—beliefs that came from our parents, from our peers, from our teachers, from the culture and society surrounding us. Often we don't even realize that these beliefs aren't necessarily ours until we stop and look at them a little harder, dig a little deeper. Maybe we have a subconscious (or even a conscious) belief that "talent" is the only road to success. Maybe we automatically assume we aren't talented in a certain area so we don't even set foot there. Is talent real? Maybe. Is it only talent that will allow you to achieve something great? Absolutely not. It's a hearty combination of passion, drive, and devoted focus. And those are all **choices** you can make.

I can remember watching figure skating during the 1988 Winter Olympics. I'd see their routines and be absolutely floored by the spins, flips, jumps, and lifts. There was no part of me that believed I could do the same thing. What I saw was choreographed perfection—three-minutes of concentrated awesomeness—and I was just a kid in his Transformer jammies watching TV. What I couldn't see was that it took an entire career's worth of energy (many failures included) to get there. Those Olympic skaters fell a thousand times before those moments on camera, but they kept making the choice to do it again. A *lot* of effort goes into making something look effortless. I know that now.

One of the first experiences I had of working toward that kind of effortlessness was with juggling. I was introduced to the art form when I was a Bob-Marley-T-shirt-wearing, long-haired hippie dude in my early 20s. I was headed home after a drum circle downtown in the square, djembe drum over my shoulder in all its glory, and I happened to take a shortcut through the park to get to my jeep. I saw this guy juggling, and he was in the zone, focused on nothing but tossing and catching. I had seen juggling before, but I didn't think I was capable of doing it. In that moment, a switch was flipped in my brain. My free-spirited, bohemian interest was piqued, and I realized I had the potential if I just put in the time and energy.

He was nice enough to show me the basics and let me try it out for myself. I was immediately hooked. My hyper-focus (a product of my ADHD) kept me up all night, literally, working on this new juggling skill. At 7am the next morning, my dad, a professor in Biochemistry at the University of Georgia, came out into the carport on his way to work to find me at the end of my all-night juggling "immersion." I had forgotten to sleep, and I was still pulsing with exhilaration. My brilliantly science-minded father asked what I was doing, baffled by my energy level so early in the morning. I was grinning madly like a six-year-old who just devoured his whole bag of Halloween candy as I told him that I'd been up all night learning to juggle. "Do you want me to teach you?" I asked. He shook his head and laughed as he got into his car. He was headed to the lab to do serious things, I'm sure, like mixing gases in precise ways so they don't explode and pouring dangerous liquids into beakers and stuff like that. Science-y things.

The point (other than the fact that I can get a little obsessive at times) is that I spent at least 12 hours straight that night dropping balls. But I *chose* to keep picking up the balls and doing it again. I continued to practice for years (and I still do). Only after hundreds of hours did I get to the point where people could see me juggle and say, "You make it look so easy."

Challenges and roadblocks appear for all of us, whether it's the monotony of picking up dropped balls or the conflict of time management. Sometimes it's that we're afraid of being vulnerable or that we have a lack of confidence. Many of us have days where we feel like we're not good enough, smart enough, or *talented* enough. Sometimes we're lazy and just find it easier to sit on the couch and watch TV. Some of us think we're "too old." (What does that even mean?!) I'd invite you to reframe your thinking: **Obstacles of inconvenience can be opportunities.**

I once suffered from tendonitis in my right arm so severely that I had to put it in a sling for two months. I'm right-handed and had very limited motion with that side, so I couldn't write. Instead of complaining and stressing about it, I saw it as an opportunity to learn how to write with my left hand. Hurdles are meant to be jumped. (I know, I've seen this in the Olympics too!)

Taking action is just a decision you make. It's moving from "wanting to do" to "doing." **The choices we make today dictate the people we become tomorrow.** So who do you want to become? It's my intention to help you become a better *you*. A greater you, a stronger you, a richer you, a healthier you. Be excited about what you are capable of achieving. Be *bold* and be real. This is what life is about.

SIX SLICES OF BAMERONI PIZZA

Before this method was officially a method (meaning before I had given names to the six steps and organized all this information), I had used it to learn juggling, drumming, speaking Swiss-German, and even to lose 87 pounds. I didn't purposefully use a methodology, but when I looked back on those experiences, I could see that all the BAM ingredients were in place.

It's a formula that has consistently worked well for me. I'm currently traveling the world using those skills, and I have been able to create a career that I love based upon them. You can use the method to learn virtually any skill you want to learn, and I believe that if you truly want to accomplish something, you can—regardless of your past, your circumstances, your race, gender, age, or income. So I want to share my tasty recipe with you. Sound good?

The six components are not linear steps. Yes, you can go from one to the next in the order that they're listed. But you don't just finish one step, be done with it, and then move on to the next. Each piece has an impact on the other pieces. They feed off of each other, they are interrelated, and they evolve throughout the process. You'll constantly be working on most of them at the same time. **These are the six components of the Bold Achievement Method:**

1. Wake Up Your Mind.
2. Shake Up Your Thinking.
3. Round Up Your Crew.

4. Set Up Your Space.

5. Get Up and Go.

6. Show Up and Rock It.

Throughout each chapter, I'll share stories, suggestions, and examples as to how to make each of these work for you most effectively.

When I learned saxophone, I kept a journal of my progress. Sometimes I wrote down what I did during a practice session. Sometimes I wrote down when I was feeling particularly inspired or defeated. I made use of multiple exclamation points often!!! It was a way to ground myself out, a way I could be the first member of my own support team. I suggest you keep a journal of your learning adventure. There are no rules here; this is just another way to hold yourself accountable. Putting your thoughts into words will help bring clarity to your process.

If you want an extra nudge, I've created a **Bold Achievement Manual**—a guide that goes along with each chapter and includes questions, suggestions, and action steps to help focus your brain on your task. The Manual, plus lots of other resources, videos, and helpful information can be found at www.bamthebook.com/extras. If the crazy saxophone guy with ADHD can do it, so can you! It's like fun homework. (*I know, I didn't think that was possible either!*)

"*That's great, Bronkar. I'm ready to dive in. One question: I have this feeling that you're going to tell a lot of stories about musical instruments, juggling, and live performance. How will that apply to me and my skill if I'm not an entertainer or some-*

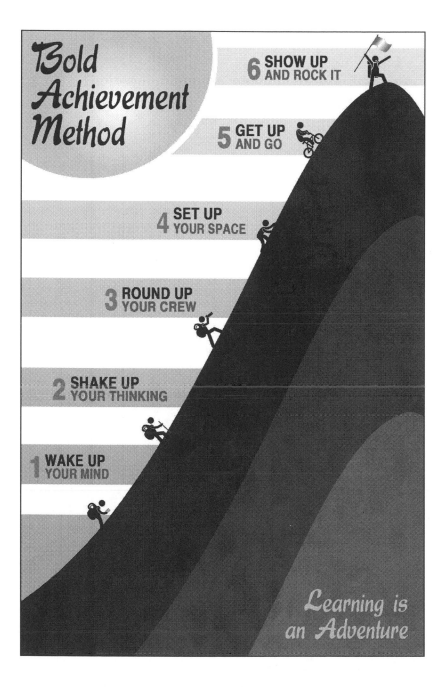

one who gets up on a stage?" Good question. I can tell you are going to be my favorite student. *wink* We put on performances every day, whether we realize it or not. The Subway employee who makes your sandwich is onstage. She sets the tone when you come into the store, creates an experience inside of her interaction with you, and has the opportunity to impact you positively or negatively. The salesperson making a call is performing. He's using his voice and his words to sell a product or service, and the spotlight comes on every time he picks up the phone. CEOs perform as they make presentations in company meetings—holding the attention of the room as they deliver information or an idea. In fact, every moment that you express yourself through your skill to the world is essentially a moment onstage. So let's get ready for showtime!

"All the world's a stage, and all the men and women merely players..."

- WILLIAM SHAKESPEARE, AS YOU LIKE IT

THE SECTION WHERE YOU IMAGINE UPLIFTING ORCHESTRAL MUSIC PLAYING BEHIND IT

Learning isn't about being the best or the greatest. Don't get caught up in that mental trap. It's doesn't have to be a competition. It's a personal evolution. You can enter a contest to get the trophy, and there's nothing owrong with that. But the act of broadening your mind and widening your capacity for knowledge is about so much more.

It's about finding your purest essence and applying it to whatever you do—whether it's learning a sport, an instrument, a computer program, a craft. My friend and former life coach Brian Poirier told me: "How you do anything is how you do everything." The skills that you learn are just mediums to express yourself through. Once you start to view it like that, your expectation for perfection changes. Success is more about fulfillment, and you become fulfilled by living your life passionately and being your most genuine self.

"Don't ask yourself what the world needs; ask yourself what makes you come alive. And then go and do that. Because what the world needs is people who have come alive."

— Howard Thurman

CHAPTER 1:

WAKE UP YOUR MIND

When I wake every day, an invisible magnetic field pulls me out of bed, toward the back door, and into the outside world of the morning. I notice the color of the sky, the mood of the earth, and the disposition of the wind. I listen for the birds that are singing their sunrise songs, and I take a deep breath to get myself in tune. I stretch my body, reaching for clouds above and then dirt below, feeling more and more released from sleep. Before this ritual is completed, my brain is foggy, I may have put my shirt on inside out, and I can make no promises about the words that come out of my mouth. After my fresh air cleanse, it's suddenly easier to get dressed, make a to-do list, and speak in complete sentences. Then I'm set up for the rest of the day.

I'm sure you've got your own morning ritual that defines you. Some people like to go for a run first thing in the morning. Some can't operate until they take a cool shower. Some people need a four-egg Denver omelet, and some don't want anything except a hot cup of coffee. Everyone's got their own routine. You probably notice that whatever you do in the morning sets the tone for the day.

There's a process of shaking off the sleep and emerging into wakefulness, and if you do it right, you feel like you can conquer anything. That's what this first step is about, waking up your mind so that you have the clarity to do all the other steps successfully. We begin the learning adventure here, and it's often necessary to revisit this step along the way to get back in line. Throughout our journey, we sometimes fall asleep and have to hit the reset button, reminding ourselves of where the path lies.

We're getting our ducks in a row, our house in order, our facts straight. We're clearing up the details so that we have a strong foundation to build on. Having gone to circus school and being immersed in that culture, I did a fair amount of acrobatics training. When I was with Circus Monti in 2006, the entire cast did an acrobatic number where we formed a human pyramid. This involved four people on hands and knees on the ground, three people who climbed on top of them to form a second layer, two people in a layer above them, and one person on the top. If the people on the bottom layer were weak, uncertain, and unprepared for the task, then the whole pyramid collapsed on itself. Not fun for anyone (especially those on the ground level). So we want our bottom

layer—in a human pyramid or in a learning process—to be confident, clear, sure, and strong.

There are five things you need to get clarity on in order to wake up your mind and build that strong foundation. They are:

1. The Now
2. The Intentions
3. The Motivations
4. The Obstacles
5. The Deadlines

THE NOW

Mindfulness is one of those words that a lot of people don't know what to do with. Like "loitering" or "censure." (*Oh, is that just me?*) People either think it's too spiritual, too hippie, too obvious, or too boring. But it's none of those things. It's just being fully aware of the present moment. You focus your complete attention only on the now—experiencing thoughts, feelings, and sensations without judgement.

It's a check-in with the self. "Hey self, how's it going? How are you feeling right now, in this moment? Are you anxious? Excited? Defeated? Determined?" Anything you're feeling is totally okay. Accepting it and acknowledging it is all you have to do. Being mindful about the moment is something you can keep coming back to throughout the process. In fact, incorporating it into everyday life will only benefit you, whether you are aiming to learn something or not.

There was a time when I thought this kind of stuff was bogus. I didn't have time to sit around thinking about my feelings! I felt like I needed to be constantly on the move. That was until two of my greatest mentors, life coaches, and favorite people in the world, Brian Poirier and Christine "CeCe" Cannavo, shared with me some really practical centering techniques focused on getting grounded and being in the moment. From their guidance, I developed my own mindfulness meditation which I do every day. I call it Back to the Basics. I first think of those things that make up our primitive needs as humans: food, water, oxygen. I acknowledge those essential resources, and I choose to live and operate from a place of gratitude, no matter what else is going on in my life. There are days I wake up feeling defeated, days when my energy is low, and some days where I feel sullen and cynical. These are the times when meditation is the absolute last thing I want to do. And these are the times when I *most* need to do it.

"Why do I need to meditate? Shouldn't I just get busy practicing my skill? Getting in tune with my emotions is not what I'm reading this book for." Trust me, grasshopper. Just go with it. It doesn't have to be sacred or spiritual or showy or mystical. **It's basic sanity maintenance.** Look, it's all about getting your head right, centering yourself for success, and yes, being in tune with your internal barometer. How you feel has a direct result on the progress you're going to make. Accepting how you feel without being ashamed, embarrassed, resentful—whatever—gives you a sense of power and ownership over yourself and those emotions. It makes

you stronger. That centeredness also helps when you start to feel the pangs of frustration during the process. And frustration plagues us all when we're changing our brain to learn something new. Getting a hold of our feelings is the first tool to battling that undesirable emotion.

When I began learning the saxophone, I had this fantasy of playing like a master, my fingers dancing up and down the instrument with perfect flow. When I played that first note, I realized that my dream scenario and current reality were grossly out of sync. The moment the sound came out, my head was clouded with doubt and insecurity. The note was reminiscent of an angry goose, squawking with a vengeance. It was loud and uncontrolled, and I was embarrassed. I felt stupid for even trying. The challenges loomed ahead of me, and I was imagining all the time I'd have to put in before I would sound less goose-like. I was beginning to second guess my decision to learn. Maybe I wasn't cut out for this instrument after all. But once I declared those feelings and owned up to them, they had no power over me anymore.

Think about your starting point, what it feels like at the beginning of this awesome journey. Recognize how cool it is that we actually have the power to make the choice to expand our minds. We have the capability to sculpt ourselves into the humans we want to be. But you already know that, don't you? I know it, too, but I still think it's kind of an amazing thought every time it surfaces.

If you really want to, you can get so much more out of this than just learning a skill. It doesn't have to be only about fulfilling the bottom line and checking something off your list. This journey can allow you to discover the tools to unlock your truest you, help you channel that into your goals and have you radiating at your highest frequency. It can boost your confidence and build your boldness, giving you even more power to shape your life into what you want it to be.

THE INTENTIONS

I'm terrible at shopping for clothes. I hate it actually. I would rather spend the day doing algebra equations. In the desert. Dressed in a snowsuit. But I needed to get something to wear for an upcoming event. I went directly to Cyndi for help. She did something remarkable. See, I was ready to just jump in the car, go to the nearest store and grab the first thing I saw that wasn't awful. But Cyndi sat me down, asked me some questions, and led me to figure out what my intentions were for the shopping trip. "Is the event casual or formal? What's most comfortable for performing in? What colors make you feel confident and strong?" I'm pretty sure there was a golden glow above her head as I answered the questions I hadn't thought to ask myself. In five minutes I had complete clarity on what I needed and wanted. We headed to Macy's and went right for the exact pieces I needed. We finished the trip in a lot less time than I would have taken had I gone in there with no clear intention. Let's just say that without Cyndi helping me figure out what I wanted, I would have come home with a wristwatch, one of those electric foot massagers, and a bar of that Godiva chocolate they sell at the checkout register. (And I don't even wear wristwatches!)

Clear intentions are absolutely paramount to getting the result that you want. It sounds obvious, but it's so easy for some of us (I'm talking to myself here!) to just zoom off towards something shiny and not think about the reason we're on the move. Halfway there we lose interest because we have no goal. Or we move on to some other goal because we can't remember where we were going in the first place. Knowing what you want allows you to make the right choices along the journey. It allows you to not be distracted by the things that won't get you there. It keeps you focused and centered.

So do a mental fast forward to the end of your learning process. You are going to end with a result no matter what you do, but what result do you *want*? What do you see for yourself? **Visualize** what success looks like to you. See yourself giving that speech, playing that guitar, growing that garden, creating that website, etc. Are you smiling? Are you happy? What time of day is it? What clothes are you wearing? Who's there with you? How does it feel? **When it's real to you, everything along the way has much more meaning.**

With saxophone, I had four extremely clear goals, and I made it a point to write them out in my journal. They were: 1) to incorporate the saxophone into my one-man show; 2) to be able to express myself fully through the instrument; 3) to be able to play an instrument that would continually encourage me to learn and grow, that I would never have complete mastery over; and 4) to be able to communicate with others and create happiness and joy in them through music.

When I looked a little deeper at each intention, something else became clear to me. Each of my specific goals was not that much different than anyone else's. My first intention was about **career enhancement**, second was **self-expression**, third was **personal development**, and fourth was **serving others**. My guess is that your true motivation for learning a skill is about at least one of these, if not all. Breaking it down to this basic understanding brought another level of clarity to me that only strengthened my resolve to accomplish my objectives. And knowing specifically what my goals were allowed me to focus my energy where it needed to go, instead of wasting it in pointless directions.

The more precise and coherent you are in stating your destination, the faster you will get there. This affects every other decision and choice you make along the way. When you get distracted, coming back to your intentions will pull you back on the path. Do you have goals? (*Hint: The answer is yes!*) Great! Then grab a piece of paper right now. Write down your intentions and goals and post them where you can see them everyday. You can scrap this paper and revise your goals anytime, but doing it now is an easy step in the right direction.

THE MOTIVATIONS

Several years ago, I convinced Cyndi to learn how to juggle. She had made several half-hearted attempts over the years before that first success moment. Her thought process was mostly, "This would be something kind of cool to know how to do." Basically just to be able to say she *could*. She didn't really care about the art of it. She just wanted to have that ability tucked away on her list of "cool party tricks." And just to be clear, she probably does have an actual document on her computer titled "Cool Party Tricks."

Anyway, she finally got to add that one to her list. But once she got the three-ball basic juggling pattern down, that was it. She was done. She had no desire to go any further. In all of our years together, I've urged her every so often to keep working on it, telling her she could do it if she just tried. And she always tells me, "I just don't *want* to do it."

Her motivation to juggle was weak. She could take it or leave it. But I am mesmerized by the art of it and intoxicated by the mental challenge it provides. I love that it brings my eye-hand coordination to new levels. It's physical activity, but emotional therapy. It's a moving meditation for me. My motivation to learn was real and it went deep.

Your level of motivation dictates where the threshold is for giving up. Low (and shallow) motivation and you're likely to give up at the slightest obstacle. The moment you have to put in just a *little bit more* effort is the moment you call it a day. Higher (and more pure) motivation changes the way you look at the obstacles. You want what's on the other side of them more fiercely. They seem less intimidating. Or maybe you're just more willing to walk into the fire.

Finding your true motivation is the only way you're going to succeed in learning a skill to the best of your ability. You simply won't get that far if you have no reason to. Sure, you can be motivated **by** others, but when they're gone, oftentimes so is the motivation. It has to be within you, it has to be real, and it has to go deep. This real motivation will be your body armor when you're battling roadblocks, resistance, failures, and vulnerabilities.

Think about what your true motivations are for learning your skill. It could be: "I want to garden because I want my children to know where real food comes from and to make healthy choices." "I want to learn ukulele so I can strum it around the campfire at our family reunion and get everyone singing to bring us closer together." "I want to learn PowerPoint so I can improve my presentations so I can get that promotion to buy my husband that boat that he's always dreamed about."

I encourage you to dig for the real motivation, and I encourage you to uncover the passion inside of you that radiates outward. Lead with that. The part of you that glows. The part of you that sings. Your essence. Apply that bright, luminous piece of you to everything that you do. Live from the inside out, not the other way around.

THE OBSTACLES

Cyndi and I had all the excuses in the world not to jump into the giant project of writing a book. Everyone tells you that the first few months of having a baby is the hardest time on a relationship. If you're a parent, you understand what I mean. The first few months are chaos. A full night's sleep is something you would daydream about if you had time or brainpower to daydream. Adjusting to this new little person being inserted into your daily life is something you just can't possibly prepare for, no matter how many books you read, videos you watched, or how much googling you did on the internet. Yet the inspiration to start writing came when our son Elijah was just around 8 weeks old.

There were plenty of moments where quitting would have been easier. And actually not even starting seemed like the *smart* and *rational* thing to do. On top of that, Cyndi had freelance jobs she was trying to squeeze in, and I was taking gigs that I could have said no to. These were the roadblocks to us finishing our book. And we had choices to make. Cyndi quit her freelance jobs to focus only on the book. I stopped taking the unimportant gigs. But we had to create a system that worked for us to give Elijah all the love and attention he needed while simultaneously putting energy toward our business and our book.

Some obstacles you can knock down and get rid of, and some you have to figure out how to climb over, detour around, or cut through. There will **always** be challenges, bumps along the way, and hurdles to overcome. And what's more, **everyone** has them. No one is immune, no matter how easy you think they have it. When you identify the obstacles, they don't have as much power over you, and you can figure out how to conquer them.

THE DEADLINES

Making a timeline for learning your skill can encourage you to work harder than you would otherwise. With saxophone, I looked at my calendar and picked a specific performance at which I planned to debut the instrument. With juggling, I was offered a gig as soon as I started learning. (I was hardly qualified in that moment, but I said yes!) In writing this book, I was hired for a speaking engagement with a nationwide company and pre-sold 220 copies to them—before it was even written. I literally *signed a contract* that demanded I finish my book!

While you may not be locked into learning with a legal document, it is important to make it real. Set a deadline to achieve your goals by. We have project deadlines at work, we have due dates for our bills, some of us even have car maintenance done on a specific schedule. If we're serious about learning a skill, we should treat it the same way.

Create a deadline and attach your specific intentions to it. Treat it like a professional project you're getting paid for and make milestones to reach along the way. The key here is making it tangible and concrete. When someone says, "I want to learn guitar," and that's the extent of it, there's no specific goal. And who's to say when "learning guitar" is actually achieved? Do they want to learn three chords? Do they want to be able to play five songs? Do they want to be able to rock a solo like Jimi Hendrix? Be specific and put it on your calendar.

∽

Learning a new skill is a lot more than just the physical *doing*. Waking up your mind, engaging your brain, and uncovering the whys, whats, and hows will bring vitality to your process in amazing ways. You can (and should) come back to this step often to refresh and reset. Goals and motivations can change, new obstacles can appear, and deadlines can shift. Wipe the fog from the lens of your consciousness and you will make the rest of your journey fuller and more alive.

"You can often change your circumstances by changing your attitude."
– Eleanor Roosevelt

CHAPTER 2:

SHAKE UP YOUR THINKING

In the early 90s, I had a pair of acid washed jeans, black, with three belt loops on either side of the front, and four rockin' pleats creating that extra bloated look we all loved. I begged my mom for these jeans, and when I wore them I felt two levels more popular than I was. If I were feeling especially trendy, I'd tight roll the pant legs up a few inches and slouch down my white socks around the ankles. I thought this was the coolest I could possibly be. Why would I ever want to wear anything else? Nothing could change my mind... except time.

I had a strong belief that couldn't be shaken, and yet fast forward ten years and I'm looking at pictures of myself thinking, "Oh wow. That poor kid." Our unshakable beliefs *can* and *do* shift. Thoughts that we adhere to so stubbornly evolve into new and different thoughts, sometimes totally opposite from what they were before. We can firmly take a position that we believe to be right, and later think that same belief to be wrong. Crazy, right?!

Being passionate about an idea is awesome. It's how we make progress in our world. It's how we make discoveries and improve lives. But so is being receptive to other ideas. Being open to the fact that we aren't perfect, our worldviews aren't always true, our sight isn't always 20/20—this is real genius. This is how exceptional advancements are made. I invite you to make three changes in your point of view about learning and about yourself, in order to make better, faster, and more progress in your learning journey.

1. Succeed by failing.
2. Think like a baby.
3. Create your new identity.

SUCCEED BY FAILING

In 2011, I got a phone call from the casting director of the TV show *America's Got Talent*. They offered to fly me into Los Angeles to be on their show. I would be bypassing the open auditions—where any and everyone could line up and do their act for the casting directors—and go straight to the auditions filmed in front of a live audience for the show's famous judges—Piers Morgan, Sharon Osbourne, and David Hasselhoff.

As I was on the call, a movie was playing through my head: I show up at the auditions, everyone backstage sees me warm up, and they are immediately wowed. The host of the show approaches and pulls me off to the side, telling me how talented I am and how it's a no-brainer that I'll win. The judges are speechless, won over by my flawless routine, praising my every move. I win the show and become a household name. My career is ignited, I've reached the top, and life is complete.

My ego was a super-sized balloon that didn't think it could be popped. I really believed I knew what I was walking into, that I was clearly the best performer they would see, and that it would be an easy win. (*Those pleated jeans are the best!*)

The show works like this: Each act has a maximum of 90 seconds to perform for the judges. Each judge has a buzzer, and there's a giant X that corresponds to each buzzer over the stage. At any point during your performance, if a judge decides they're over it and they don't want you to advance to the next round, they press their buzzer, making the ultimate "you lose" sound effect and lighting up the X. It's really over-dramatic. If all three judges buzz you, then you're out. Afterwards they comment on your act as you stand completely exposed in the middle of the enormous stage.

The taping day is an all-day affair, and long before we ever set foot on the stage, the producers are meeting with us and deciding what "character" they want us to be for the show. There's very little reality involved in reality TV. I knew this was how these shows worked, but in my mind, this was going to be different. They wanted to portray me as the mysterious, unknown wild card, keeping my beatbox juggling act a secret until I got on the stage. I felt uneasy about this contrived portrayal. I just wanted to get out there and show the crowd and the judges the skill I had been working on for years.

Despite the fact that it felt wrong, the voice in my head said, "Think how cool it would be if you won, dude!" My ego ignored my gut, and I followed the producers' lead. Before my grand entrance, the host, Nick Cannon, was asking me interview questions backstage. I was a ball of nervous energy—palms sweating, heart pounding, pulse racing.

They introduced me, and I ran out onto the colossal stage in front of the judges and the live audience. The cameras were rolling, lights were blazing, and a fearful voice inside my head said, "You'd better be amazing or you're going to look like a fool." After a few questions from the judges, I sank into the routine I had prepared. I didn't feel grounded. Doubt and insecurity were filling my ego balloon. Ten seconds in, I heard the first X buzz. It was blaring louder than my own microphone volume. I tried to ignore it and keep my focus, but the next X came before I could gather my thoughts. I didn't even finish my routine before I got the third and final X. This was not at all like I visualized.

The judges were not impressed. They said I could pass as a street performer at best, but certainly not as a national TV star. Instead of the ultimate validation, I experienced the ultimate failure. I fell flat on my face, humiliated. My ego balloon had burst into shrunken, rubbery pieces. The routine played on repeat in my head, trapping me in that moment of embarrassment.

I had a choice to make. I could swear off doing TV ever again. In fact, I could swear off doing public performances ever again. If I never put myself out there for the world to judge, then I would be protected from disappointment about what they had to say

The other option was to look a little deeper, past my

comfort level, and figure out why I really failed. Why didn't it go as I had visualized? And that's what I chose to do. It's not that I was *good* or *bad*, right or wrong. It's that I wasn't prepared for that particular opportunity. I had done thousands of live shows before, but never on TV and never on the premise of being judged.

The way I looked at my own performance would have to change in order for me to be successful. I worked hard to create more television appearances so that I could eliminate that weakness. I got more and more experience. It got easier every time I did it. I made notes, graciously accepted feedback and continuously tweaked my approach until I felt confident in the world of TV.

Three years later, I opened for Justin Willman (host of the show *Cupcake Wars*) at Club Nokia in Los Angeles. The producers for *The Tonight Show with Jay Leno* were in the audience, and they approached me afterward to see if I wanted to be a guest on the show. It was the big moment I had been working toward! They wanted me to do my beatbox juggling (the very performance that had been rejected on *America's Got Talent*), and they gave me a week to create a customized holiday piece for a Christmas-themed show.

When the day of the taping came, I could feel those old emotions rising to the surface. The fear and doubt were pushing on my chest again, trying to break out, but I didn't give in to them. I was prepared. I knew what to expect. I knew who the audience was and how to play to the camera. All the energy I put into doing TV shows over the last few years—energy that resulted from my intense failure—was being recirculated into a much more positive experience. I performed my routine with confidence to a cheering crowd and a highly impressed Jay Leno.

The word failure has so many negative connotations. We grow up believing we have to avoid it. It means we didn't win. We lost. We're inadequate. Except that everyone ever in the history of everybodies has experienced it. Especially those people who succeed big. My educated guess is that they also failed really big. It's not mud. Don't sink into it and get stuck there. It's a trampoline. Every time you hit the lowest point, you have an opportunity to then make it to your highest. Our biggest leaps are often made after our greatest failures.

I spoke with my friend, two-time Olympic gymnast and memory expert Lance Ringnald, about his experience with failure and success. In the gym, falling and failing is just a normal part of the process. They are constantly attempting flips, jumps, and tumbles, and the only way to learn it is to do it. With each mistake, they learn something right away about what they were doing wrong and what they could do to correct it. He put it this way: "Every time you fall, it's one less fall before you master that trick."

I felt a similar way about learning to juggle. The process is mostly dropping and picking up balls. If I had to guess, I'd say it's 99% failure and 1% success. I had to really get comfortable with my imperfections while I was learning. I had to have a sense of humor about it and let go of expectations. I also learned to take on a more cosmic perspective to deal with any frustrations I had. I'd zoom out and look at the universe and realize, "I'm not really that big of a deal and neither is this moment." Thinking about something way bigger than I am helped me ground out.

Failure should be a daily event. It has to be viewed as getting us one step closer to succeeding. Think about the last big mistake you made. Were you quick to put it behind you or did you get up close and personal with it to discover the lesson within? There's something valuable inside of every error made. If you don't see it right away, crack it open and look harder. And then get back into action. Be okay with imperfection. If you're not failing, you're not learning. If you go into the process knowing that, then it's a little bit less intimidating.

THINK LIKE A BABY

The really great thing about writing this book with a newborn in the house was that over the span of just a few short months I witnessed a massive amount of growth, learning and change take place in this tiny human's life. Watching Elijah learn skill after skill for the first time provided a whole lot of insight into the learning process. He continuously attempts the impossible until it becomes possible.

I travel a lot for my work as a speaker and unfortunately, it sometimes requires me being away from Cyndi and Elijah for a week at a time. I remember leaving for one event, and when I said goodbye and walked out the door, Elijah was an immobile baby. He would stay where you put him when you put him down. We could sit next to him on the floor in the mornings and place our hot cups of coffee down next to us and relax quietly while he sat and inspected every detail of his squishy stacking rings or laid on his tummy laughing at the baby in the mirror in front of him. When I returned from six days away, that baby had morphed into a completely different baby. He would inchworm his way across the room to whatever caught his eye. Coffee cups were banned from the floor from this day forward.

I was majorly bummed to have missed the transition and the actual moment where he went from stationary to moving, but more than that, I was baffled at how it could happen so fast! When I analyzed the situation more deeply, I realized that he wasn't really learning at a superhuman rate. He was putting every ounce of his energy all day (and sometimes all night, *sigh*) into his new skills. Later, when he learned to pull up to standing, he would spend all day every day pulling up, sitting down, pulling up, sitting down. The amount of effort put in was astonishing. He would wake in the night pulling up on the crib. I'm pretty sure he was also dreaming about pulling up and sitting down (probably in a swimming pool filled with banana pureé). When he crawled over to us so sweetly for a hug, we realized it wasn't for a hug at all, it was so he could pull his little body up to standing on our arms or legs. Sneaky kid.

We all come into the world with this insane amount of persistence. It allows us to learn to crawl, roll over, grab things, walk, speak—everything! No amount of falls keeps us from getting back up and trying to stand again. When we can't quite roll over onto our tummies, we keep reaching over our shoulder over and over again until we develop

Elijah, the first time he pulled himself to standing - July 2016

enough coordination to do it. It doesn't occur to us to just stop trying. It doesn't even occur to us that these instances would be failures.

One of my friends and mentors, Bill Barr, is a wonderful example of a human being putting the baby perspective into practice. He says that "each effort is a partial success in its own way." Every time we reach for something (as a baby does) and we don't quite hit our target, we are building synapses and pathways. It's like majestic cities of knowledge being constructed in our brains. Eventually our goal is achieved, but these prior efforts are a necessary part of the process and so, therefore, are little successes on their own.

We have perpetual curiosity as babies, too. Every object is thrilling. Electrical outlets—riveting! The remote control—captivating! A measuring cup—wildly fascinating! And not just one time, but for days on end. Every day we look at the same things with seemingly new eyes. Babies have a wonderful sense of humor about themselves, they are determined and inspired, and they are incredibly focused.

Babies are the perfect example of what it's like to be in a constant learning mode. Typically, the recommendation in life is to **NOT** act like a baby. But I'm suggesting you do the opposite. Be a baby! Be curious about the world around you, viewing things like you've never seen them before. Laugh at yourself and find the fun in whatever you do. Allow yourself to get in the zone and stay there for a while. Be insanely persistent, unfazed by challenges, and driven to succeed no matter what.

CREATE YOUR NEW IDENTITY

There's you now. And there's the you of the future—the new you. This new you has achieved the goals set by the old you. You of the now is awesome, for sure. But you of the future wow! That you is wiser, happier and more confident. You

2.0. This you has a new skill tucked under the belt. Don't *wait* to be this new you. Talk like the new you would talk. Act like the new you would act. Become that new you in the world. Embrace it.

When I first started learning saxophone, I decided to share it with the world by posting a photo to Facebook. I was announcing that I was this new version of me—the version that is a sax player. It sounds simple. But it took a lot for me to click "Post." I typed the caption, attached the picture and stared at the screen. I edited the text continuously, dragging it out so I didn't have to share it just yet. I felt so nervous. And I was embarrassed that I was nervous! But what if people had some new expectation of me to be awesome at the saxophone? And what if they find out I'm NOT awesome?! About six times, I tried closing out the browser and got the message, "Are you sure you want to leave this page?" Was I sure?! Am I the kind of person that just leaves and gives up?! Aaaaahhhhh! It was so uncomfortable.

When I finally summoned the nerve to post it, I was immensely relieved to see responses of enthusiasm and excitement. Yes, they did have this new expectation for me to be a saxophone player. But it was with support and love. I immediately got a message from my friend, Shoehorn, a master tap dancing sax player who had toured the world for years as a professional musician. He saw I needed support and offered to give me a lesson. I got personal notes of encouragement from friends and family. Text messages came in with thumbs-up emojis. (Also a couple pizza emojis, which I took as a good sign.) There was so much love and energy circulating back to me as a direct result of putting myself in that super vulnerable position. It was powerful. And now I was fully committed. I saw myself as a sax player, I told the world I was a sax player, and now the world recognized me as a sax player.

We are all just human beings applying ourselves to different skills, crafts and careers. We take the essence of who we are at the core and channel it into whatever we desire. We have a choice! No one is *born* a scientist or a teacher or a world-class pianist. These are roles we choose. I am a drummer, a father, a son, a hiker, a spaghetti-lover, a connector, a speaker—many things. I decided to BE a saxophone player as well.

Telling people what you're doing also creates accountability with them. (This is an essential part of the process that we will dig into more in the next chapter.) You do create an expectation, but it's a really good one. *Be* what you are learning how to be. It's surprising how much that simple thought change affects your attitude and how much your attitude in turn affects your process. Putting your "new identity" out into the world impacts who and what you attract.

More opportunities come your way, and it's literally the fact that you are telling people about what you're doing. People know what you need, and they're able to offer you support.

Before you go out and tell the world, tell **yourself**. Own it. And when you do say it out loud, eliminate the word "try." None of this: "I'm going to try and learn..." Our words hold weight. If we say something enough we'll believe it. Adding in "try" is giving yourself permission to bail. Don't give yourself that easy out. As Yoda says in *Empire Strikes Back*: "Do. Or do not. There is no try." And there's nothing like a *Star Wars* quote to close out a chapter.

"Each friend represents a world in us, a world possibly not born until they arrive, and it is only by this meeting that a new world is born."
— Anais Nin

CHAPTER 3:

ROUND UP YOUR CREW

I've unpacked a moving truck alone. I've set up a ten-person tent alone. I've painted a house alone. None of these things were fun. In fact, they were all supremely *unfun*. I scratched some of the moved furniture. My tent blew over several times before I got it up. And my back was a total wreck after the first coat of paint. Doing stuff alone sucks.

And it's not just that it's exhausting, boring and/or backbreaking. You literally cannot do as much, make it as far, or do it as well as you can when you have that support team behind you. Your squad. Your troop. Your crew. When it comes to learning something new, if you have no outside help, your learning is totally one-sided. You have no new perspectives, no one cheering you from the sidelines, and no one to keep you in check and on track.

Some of you may be saying to yourself, "Oh, but I'm an introvert," or, "I work better solo." And that may be true. But you **can** be an introvert, work solo, enjoy *me-time*, and still benefit from having others in your life to support you. In fact, no one is exempt from needing encouragement and guidance.

The people we surround ourselves with are the people that we become. If you hang around lazy people who never move from their couches and can't bear to part with their remote controls, you will probably be stuck sitting next to them watching reruns of *The Bachelor*. (*Oh the horror!*) On the flipside, if you hang around people working passionately towards their goals, you will most likely be determined and purposeful as well. Our peers influence us, for better or worse, so it's okay to be selective in choosing who you join forces with. Choose those who will lift you up, encourage you, and inspire you to be better.

It's good to take inventory of your strengths and weaknesses as you go into assembling your crew. Having flaws or shortcomings isn't a bad thing. It just means you're human. Nobody is amazing at everything. Most successful people I know have simply recognized their weaknesses and then attracted people to them who are really good at things they are not. Let's say you're having a barbecue with friends, potluck-style, and you make killer guacamole. Everyone who tries it asks for your recipe because they've never had any guacamole so amazing. Your friend Bob calls you up and says, "Can I bring guacamole to the potluck?" *Well, no, Bob, that would be silly. We all know you make terrible guacamole, and I already have that covered.* You don't say that, of course. But you do say, "Actually Bob, could you bring some of that super tasty sweet potato pie that you do so well?" Because Bob really does make a super tasty pie, and you are really bad at making desserts, but you need dessert to have a well-rounded potluck spread. Do you get where I'm going with this? You want the people on your support team who make the tasty pie that you can't make. (By the way, Cyndi says the secret to killer guacamole is mixing the avocados with salsa verde and mangoes. No one actually asks *me* to cook anything. That would be crazy.)

Your support crew also consists of the people who are going to hold you accountable for your journey. You will answer to these people. That sounds scary and ominous, but it's exactly the opposite. They are there to nudge you in the right direction, push you a little bit farther than you thought you could go, and be a motivation for you to keep going when you just feel like crashing down into a really long unnecessary nap.

It doesn't have to be overwhelming to assemble your crew. In fact, you probably already have some of them in your corner. I look at it kind of like I would if I were casting a movie. There are five roles I aim to fill:

1. The Friend
2. The Peer
3. The Instructor
4. The Cheerleader
5. The Mentor

You don't have to fill them all at once, and you don't have to have them all in order to get started. Remember, this is a journey, an adventure, a process. You may start off with one or two supporters and gather a few more along the way, or you may have already hit the jackpot and you're starting out with everyone you need.

You may not ever fill all the roles, and that doesn't mean you won't be successful. I do think you may be able to go farther and probably be more well-rounded in your skill if you do have at least one of each. But don't let it stop you if you can't find someone to fill one of the specific roles. You could have multiple people who fill one role. And you could have a person that fits into more than one category. It's not uncommon to have overlap. A Friend could be a Mentor; a Peer could be a Cheerleader; an Instructor could be a Friend. The rules are loose; it's having the supporters there that matters.

THE FRIEND

I met one of my closest friends, Sam Rogers, at the International Body Music Festival in Oakland, California in 2008. We instantly connected over our love of body percussion, beatboxing, and music. For several years now, we have been checking in with each other nearly every week. We talk about life, projects, art, music, dreams, business, and finances. We share both successful moments and personal struggles. We can be totally transparent with each other because we've built our bond as friends over the years. This allows us to support each other in the most authentic and effective way. When I

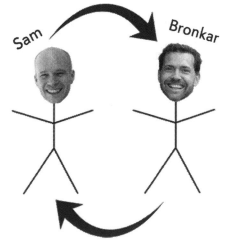

create a new learning goal for myself, Sam is one of the first people I tell about it.

Out of the five types of support crew, this is the one you're most likely to have already. They're on your team without you having to ask. All you have to do is tell them about your goal. They know you are working towards accomplishing something new so they can check in with you about your progress whenever you talk.

It's really a simple way to create accountability. And because I have a penchant for combined words (like "spork"— what a great word!), I call this person an *accountabilibuddy*. It's reciprocal. Sam is on my support crew, and I'm on his. You've got to give in order to get. When we check in, we help each other set timelines and mini-goals. We brainstorm ways to break through our challenges. Sometimes we are just there to listen to each other. It's invaluable.

accountabilibuddy
/*uh*-koun-t*uh*-bil-i-buhd-ee/

noun
A buddy that holds you accountable in exchange for you holding them accountable

Sam also gives me truly honest feedback, and I'm grateful for that because it means he's sincere about helping me get better at whatever I'm doing. You don't need the Friend to worship the ground you walk on and tell you that everything you do is gold. They give you a good ol' pat on the back sometimes, but they also aren't afraid to give you a little push. The Friend is perpetually on your side, making your journey brighter, deeper, and full of richness.

THE PEER

When I began my sax-o-matic adventure, the Peer role was filled by one of my best friends, Aaron Williams, aka Afro Ninja. Aaron and I met during a TEDx event in Los Angeles. We were both set to perform, met backstage, and made a spontaneous decision to collaborate live during the event, with no prior rehearsal. He was a tap dancer and I was a beatboxer—both percussive art forms—so it was a natural collaboration. Afterwards, our friendship flourished. I learned that Aaron was insanely talented at many other things besides tap dancing, including marimba, percussion, and piano.

sax-o-matic
/saks-o-mat-ik/

adjective
Funky and automatically saxy

BAMOLOGY DEFINITION

While I was learning sax, Aaron was taking up juggling. We checked in and encouraged each other, but the really cool thing was that Aaron had a strength that was my weakness. My natural learning style is total-immersive, extroverted, and hands-on. I'm extremely present in the moment and I have few inhibitions. I like to get out there and improvise in the world. It's an asset because I can easily jump into a situation and make myself at home, but the downside is that I'm not so great at creating strategy and concentrating on the basic processes. I'm not a highly organized person by nature, and I often overlook the finer details. Something like learning to read music is similar to dying a slow and painful death for me. Sitting still and memorizing the placement of little circles on a graph of lines sounds like a nightmare. *Treble clefs, no!! Decrescendos?! Aaaahhh!!* My natural inclination is to skip that part and just wing it. Yet I know that educating myself about the written language of music would be very beneficial to my learning of a melodic instrument, and when it does come time for me to get out there and do it in the real world, I will be more confident and flexible.

Aaron is a music teacher, so he has a wealth of knowledge on music theory. He's also a different kind of learner than I am. He's analytical, patient, and a more scientifically-minded thinker. All those things that I am not-so-great at, he does exceedingly well. So we used this as an opportunity to trade skills. I taught him to juggle in exchange for his teaching me music theory.

Because we were both learning a new skill at the same time, we created those check-ins with each other. We would text every day just to make sure we were keeping up with our rehearsals. When you're in learning mode, you need to be around others who are there, too. It makes it easier. We were accountabilibuddies, and we kept each other on top of our games. I could easily have gotten derailed without him.

This is why joining some type of club or group related to your skill can be so valuable. You're surrounded by peers on a similar path, and often you start out as strangers but become really great friends. Cyndi had this experience right after Elijah was born. One of our biggest learning adventures in life so far has been becoming parents, and one can't deny that being a new mom is way more daunting than being a new dad. So Cyndi joined a group for first-time moms. They shared stories, advice, encouragement, laughter, and tears. They created relationships that will no doubt last forever. They learned things they could never get from a book, and more importantly, they weren't *alone* on their journeys.

But it's not just a support system that Peers are good for. Two people working together to realize a shared goal is a collaboration. If you are learning the same skill, why not work on it together? Practice together, learn together, and push each other farther. Two people who create something good individually have the potential to create something exponentially greater when they work together.

I practiced saxophone with other musicians (my peers) as much as I could. Not only was it fun, but I always walked away having learned something totally new. Working with someone on my support team gave me permission to step outside of my comfort zone. It was okay if I took chances, and it was okay if I made mistakes. It's all about saying yes to the moments of opportunity. It's not always easy and it's not always comfortable, but it is very simple.

A journey is always more interesting when you have a travel buddy. I've never had a super memorable road trip by myself. Really a solo road trip is just a chunk of time spent in a car getting from one place to the next. But a trip with someone else is an opportunity to turn up the music, roll down the windows, and sing loud.

THE INSTRUCTOR

Unfortunately, you can't learn a new skill with good vibes alone, unless your desired skill is embracing hippie culture to its fullest extent. An aspiring helicopter pilot has to learn what all the cockpit buttons and knobs do. (I'm assuming there are buttons and knobs in a cockpit, right?!) An aspiring singer needs to learn how to breathe from the diaphragm. An aspiring author has to learn to write words real good and make grammar stuff happen at its bestest. *See what I did there? *wink, smile.**

People teach themselves how to do things all the time, and there's something very admirable about that. But it's less about being admirable and more about being well-rounded that really matters. By getting different perspectives from different teachers, you are really opening up the world of whatever your desired skill is.

A teacher can be a person in a room with you, who you pay for a set amount of time to instruct you in the techniques. They can be the leader of a class you attend, where you are one in a group of many students. They can also be an online presence. YouTube is a major venue for knowledge acquisition these days. At least it is as I write this in 2016. (If you are reading my book and it's 2056, and you are wondering what YouTube is, then, yay! I'm glad that our book is still doing so well.) I'd go as far as to say a teacher can also be a book on the subject or articles you find online. I'm definitely an advocate for a teacher who is live and in person, but that's not always possible. So take what you can get.

Instructors should be able to give you techniques, tips, and advice specifically related to the practice of your skill. If they are a live person with whom you can interact, they will critique you on what you're doing and help you improve. This is useful for a lot of types of skills because if you have no teacher, you may teach yourself how to do something the wrong way. If it's something physical you're doing, you may injure yourself. If you're learning a language, you may pronounce a word wrong and for your entire life be saying something like "dirt" when what you mean to say is "pie." Imagine the misunderstandings—and/or stomach aches—that could cause!

Some people will become a professional in their skill with only ever having one teacher, but if you're like I am, you want to view your skill from multiple angles. Having a wide variety of teachers means I get multiple perspectives and a more well-rounded knowledge. I get different take-aways from a live one-on-one session than I do from a You-Tube tutorial. However, both can be worthwhile.

Teachers and instructors have tremendous power, and it's important to note that as much as they can inspire and ignite, the *wrong* kind of teacher can demotivate and defeat. In middle school, I played recreational basketball. It was fun, healthy, and a great way for me to learn how to work with a team. But our coach hated his job, and when I made a mistake during practice one day, he blew up. Anger possessed him and I got an earful of reasons I wasn't fit to play on his team. In one single moment, my desire to play the sport was squashed by one person with a negative attitude. That was the last basketball practice I ever went to. So be selective about who you choose to teach you.

My friend and mentor Bill Forchion (founder of the New England Center for Circus Arts and former Cirque du Soleil acrobat and physical comedian) said something spot-on during a discussion we had about the power we have as teachers (and just as humans in general). He said: "We have the power to transform worlds with our words." When Bill got into the circus arts, he had a variety of acrobatic and physical movement instructors from different countries— China, Russia, Poland, Bulgaria. Their methods of teaching were all about fighting with yourself until you accomplished your goal. Until the achievement was reached, you were a failure. Bill didn't resonate with that teaching style, and it didn't translate well to the professional circus work-world. He remembers being hired for one event where the chore-ographer asked him to do the movements a certain way, and it went against the way his early instructors taught him. So he had a hard time with it. His brain was telling him that it was the *wrong* way to do it, but in fact it wasn't about right or wrong. It was what was expected of him to keep the job! So now, as a teacher himself, Bill has adopted a philosophy of affirmation—focusing not on wrong and right but on how different choices lead to different outcomes.

Make sure you pick instructors whose philosophies resonate with you. You're more likely to learn more and enjoy it more if you do.

THE CHEERLEADER

Whenever I'm having a lousy day, there's a part of me that says, "Suck it up, dude. You're a grown man and you can handle it." And there's another part of me that is six years old and scraped his knee falling off his bicycle. That part of me calls his mama. She's my Cheerleader, and she always has a band-aid for the cut.

My mom, Cheryl Lee, has forever been the president of my support crew. Remember circus school? (*Of course. How does one forget circus school?!*) My mom got me there. Once I picked up juggling, back in my early 20s, I couldn't stop. I was starting to develop a wide variety of unique skills—drumming, juggling, beatboxing—but I didn't know how to put it all together. Where some mothers would steer their sons away from something like circus arts and towards the more stable and predictable world of the 9-5, my mother did not. She could see my passion and drive, and did everything in her power to support me.

A little bit of online research led her to the Clown Conservatory program at the San Francisco Circus Center. It was all the way on the other side of the country, and it was totally crazy, but she wanted for me to find a place where my skills would be valued, honed, and expanded. She called the school, got information on how to apply, and excitedly presented the idea to me. I applied, was accepted, and made the move out West with the vice-president of my crew, Cyndi. My mom was there for 2am phone calls, sent money when times were tough, and even flew out for clown graduation with my dad.

When I succeeded, she cheered me on. When I failed, she cheered me on. And she continues to do so. There's always a piece of us that wants validation, that wants someone else to declare that we are doing a great job, that we're awesome. Cheerleaders give you encouragement when you're frustrated, unconditional support when you feel alone, pats on the back when you hit an achievement, and confidence when you're all out of it. They give you what I call *feel-good feedback*. You go to them when you need a boost. It's someone you can be vulnerable with. If this person were a food, they'd be chocolate! You don't actually need it to live, but it sure does make you happier and can give you that extra little push when you need it. With every victory I've had, there's always been a cheerleader in the wings, lifting me up.

THE MENTOR

I met one of my Mentors at the NAMM show (National Association of Music Merchants) in Anaheim, California. It's a huge yearly conference for music product retailers, and there are a lot of people networking and test-driving the latest hot products. I was a seasoned drummer and percussionist, but I was brand new to the world of saxophones—a rookie. The convention center was filled to the brim with music industry professionals who seemed to know it all, and I was suddenly overwhelmed by feelings of insecurity.

As I roamed the aisles, I came across a phenomenal player named Zack Sollitto who was demonstrating his expertise on the alto saxophone at one of the booths. He was a much better player than I was. I couldn't help but feel nervous at the thought of introducing myself. *What if he could tell I had no idea what I was talking about? What if he was arrogant or condescending?* But I needed some guidance. I realized I was projecting my feelings of insecurity on him, and I decided to get over it and go talk to him. He was humble and gracious, a regular person eager to share his knowledge. He and I ended up spending several hours at the conference hanging out and talking about saxophones. During our conversations, I found out that he reviews products for *Saxophone Magazine*, so he was able to answer endless questions from me about purchasing and caring for a horn. He took me under his wing and ended up being a major supporter on my journey.

I might have given up if it wasn't for Zack's support, specifically when I was buying the first mouthpiece for my saxophone. There was no other way for me to do it than go into a music store and try them out in person. That meant I had to play saxophone in the busy store, while other customers milled around, listening to my every note. And they weren't just "regular" people; they were musicians. I was still very much a beginner at saxophone, and the thought of playing in public made me break out in hives. I didn't know the lingo. I felt like an outsider. I had this nightmare vision of playing a few notes and everyone turning to look at me with disgusted expressions, then looking at each other and breaking out into hysterical laughter at me—the guy "pretending" to be a sax player and failing epically. I was terrified. Intimidated. Self conscious. Already humiliated, even though I hadn't even set foot in the store yet. I shared my vision with Zack and he offered to come with me. His support was monumental. He gave me a giant confidence boost just by being there.

A Mentor is the trusted guide that helps lead you on your journey. They're good at listening to you and not just giving you the answer but helping you find it for yourself. The Mentor might be a master of the skill you are trying to learn, or they might just be a wise and life-experienced navigator who believes in you and wants to offer direction. A Mentor could be an instructor of the skill, but what sets them apart from *only* being an instructor is that they can act as a counselor, confidant, and advice giver. They encourage and allow your personal growth. They've most likely been in your shoes before and can offer a new perspective to help elevate your game.

It's tough for most of us to approach a complete stranger. I tend to have a more extroverted style, and it can still be hard for me! But sometimes there's an opportunity right in front of you and you have to make a choice as to how much effort you are going to put into it. People are just people. And if they aren't interested in helping you, then you move on. Nothing is lost. Another option here is to hire a Mentor in the form of a personal or life coach. This is someone who specializes in bringing out the best in people who are willing. You could get recommendations from friends or co-workers or do some research on your own. You could also find a Mentor within your current network—someone you already know or someone within your workplace.

I love being around people who are farther along in

their journey than I am. It's both inspiring and humbling. There's a magnificent power and an overflow of wisdom in this kind of person that makes them a compelling addition to your crew.

"Vulnerability is the birthplace of innovation, creativity, and change."

– Dr. Brené Brown

CHAPTER 4:

SET UP YOUR SPACE

Saxophone rehearsal day two started out with a bang. All the knobs (on a scale of 1-10) were turned up to 11. Motivation = 11. Energy = 11. Enthusiasm = 11. A practice session in my man cave was about to begin. On this perfectly beautiful Southern California day, the sunlight beamed through my windows with heaven-like radiance, and I was ready for musical triumph. I opened the saxophone case like it was my battle sword and attached the mouthpiece. I took a deep breath and played the first few notes. With each note, my excitement was waning more and more, and my uncertainty was building like a wildfire. An ugly, messy, savage wildfire. There was absolutely nothing sexy (or saxy) about the sounds coming out of my instrument. All I could think about was my burning desire to get past the beginner stage.

I had set aside the time to rehearse, and I intended to fully focus, but the more notes that I played, the more these intrusive thoughts were seeping into my head: "Are the neighbors home, and can they hear me floundering??" "Am I going to wake Cyndi from her nap?" "Is that dog from next door barking because he thinks he hears an animal dying over here?!"

I was so worried about how my playing was affecting everyone around me. I was worried that anyone listening might be judging me, that they'd hear how bad it was and think I should just give it up. I kept trying to play more quietly, and I was self conscious about every single note coming out. My time for intense focus on the saxophone turned out to be intense focus on *everything* but. I knew I had to do something different in order to make any progress.

If only I had a place I could go where no one could hear me... [*Camera slowly zooms in on face as eyes dramatically widen and a lightbulb materializes in a thought bubble above head.*] I suddenly had a fantastic idea. I immediately went

 out and purchased several pieces of soundproofing foam and blankets, and I padded my man cave bathroom from floor to ceiling. My mission was to make it so that no sound could escape the room.

I recruited Cyndi to test out my soundproofing job by standing outside the man cave and listening to see if she could hear the saxophone. After it was approved, I proceeded to dive into my focused practice. No distracting thoughts pierced through my barriers. I wasn't

concerned about being heard or judged. I wasn't worried about disturbing the neighbors. I wasn't afraid of hitting the wrong notes anymore. My safe space was born. I named it my **Womb of Creativity.**

womb of creativity
/woom uhv kree-ey-tiv-i-tee/

noun
An emotionally secure place where ideas can flourish and skills can be cultivated

When you're at your most vulnerable, trying out new things, taking risks, making mistakes (i.e. LEARNING), you need a place where you feel safe, secure, and protected. My padded room served that purpose. Imperfections were welcome and encouraged. I actually laughed out loud at myself often, which felt so much better than cringing. It didn't seem like such a big deal anymore. I had permission to fail (And I did, over and over again. And again. And then a little more. Plus some additional mistakes.) Most importantly, my creative mind could thrive.

Getting into that open, eager learning mode can be scary when you're not a kid anymore. As adults, we often feel like we should already know everything we need to know. We don't have the time or the support we may have had when we were younger to pursue learning. It's just hard to go against the grain, deviate from the crowd and be a beginner at something again.

We have to make it *easy* for ourselves to succeed. And setting up our space to line up with our goals just makes sense. If I'm a surgeon, and I'm going to operate on a patient, I have a specific room I utilize. It's sterile and has the right lighting so that I can see what I'm doing. It has all the tools I need to perform the tasks of the surgery. There's a place for the patient to lie down, and there's room for all the machinery that tracks his vitals. (Let's hope.)

If you're serious about your process, as the surgeon no doubt is, then there are three steps to follow to set up your own space for practicing and building the skill. They are:

1. Locate your Womb of Creativity.
2. Equip yourself with the tools.
3. Get to your Zen Zone.

LOCATE YOUR WOMB OF CREATIVITY

Every skill is going to have different needs in terms of **where** you can do it. My padded room worked great for learning saxophone, but I needed something entirely different when I learned juggling. And I had even fewer spatial requirements when I learned to speak Swiss-German.

I spoke with acrobat, aerialist, hoop artist, and actor in the Broadway musical *Pippin*, Viktoria Grimmy, about her experience with creating space to practice. As an aerialist, she is always in need of a very specific type of space—a gym with padded floors and a certain type of aerial rig (e.g. trapeze or silks or a hoop). It wasn't always easy for her to find this type of space. When she was growing up in Monticello, NY there was literally no available gym space for her to practice, but she and her family were committed to her learning the skills. So her dad schmoozed the local high school into letting them use the gym after school hours, and they were able to set up her aerial rig so that she could rehearse in the evenings.

I once rented a storage space and used it to practice drums and other pieces for my one man show. Yes, a storage facility that people use to put the things they don't really need but can't bear to part with. I was rehearsing my theater show in between pods filled with boxes of Russian nesting dolls, old baseball trophies, and plaques that say, "Home is where the heart is." It was the only space nearby where I could make noise and not worry about who might hear me. (The only creatures listening in were the mice that lived in my walls.)

The type of space that is required varies from person to person and skill to skill. It might not even be a specific room in a specific building. It could very well be outside in a park, in your office, or in your kitchen. I even know people that do their best writing in their cars, speaking into a voice recorder as they drive. It's wherever you can physically AND mentally work on the skill without judgement. Maybe you're learning to sing, and it's your bathroom at 5am before anyone else is awake. Or maybe you're learning karate, and it's in your backyard after the sun has gone down. Or you're learning to give presentations, and it's in your office on your lunch break with the door locked. Or you're learning to beatbox and it's in the closet so you don't drive your wife crazy. (*What? No, that's never happened to me, I don't know what you're talking about.*) Figure out where you feel most inspired, free, and productive, and set up your Womb of Creativity there.

EQUIP YOURSELF WITH TOOLS

Remember the surgeon? My guess is he didn't say, "I want to be a surgeon, but I can't be bothered to have all those silly instruments. My kid's got some safety scissors, and they're bright pink so that's cool. And my wife sews, so I'll just grab a couple spools of her thread. And all that machinery to measure vitals just seems like a lot of extra work so I'm gonna pass on that."

You can't bake without an oven. You can't paint without a brush. You can't sew without a needle. Get the things you need to do the stuff you want to do. You're either thinking, "Well, duh. Obviously," or "Oooooh, I don't know. I have to spend money on something when I'm not sure if it's going to work out for me in the end?" Well, second-thought-thinker, I can tell you one thing. If you don't have what you need, you absolutely won't succeed. And I didn't even MEAN to make that rhyme. But it did, and even *I'm* more convinced now at how important it is.

There are basically two ways this can go down, and I'll give you the good ol' Bronkar vs. Cyndi comparison. Ladies first. The Cyndi Approach: Cyndi taught herself guitar when she was eighteen. She was in high school, and she didn't have access to a guitar, so she told her parents she was interested in learning. Her parents didn't know if this was something she'd be committed to or not, so they borrowed a guitar from a family friend. It was a basic model—nothing fancy—and it did the job. Cyndi practiced every day, and her parents realized she was going to stick with it for a long time. For her next birthday, they got her a guitar. It was still a basic model, but it was a little easier to play, and it was her own. A year later, Cyndi was still playing and had even formed a band. She upgraded her $100 model to a nicer $500 model with more of the features that she needed. A couple years later, still going strong and playing gigs, and her $500 model

CYNDI APPROACH

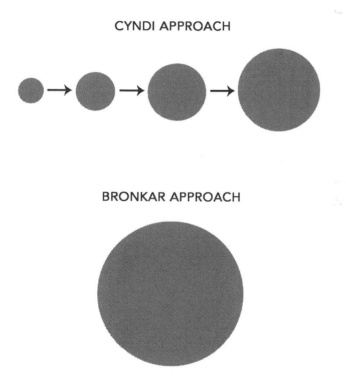

BRONKAR APPROACH

was upgraded to an even better sounding and easier playing $1500 model. She started out with a minimum investment and then increased it as her skill increased.

The Bronkar Approach: Get it all! Now! But seriously... When I went shopping for my first saxophone, I had the Cyndi Approach in mind. I was going to buy an affordable student model to start with and then upgrade later. Things were going well, I actually did buy the student model, brought it home and played it for a day, then took it back and returned it for the really nice fancy-pants model instead. I decided I needed the best one right from the start. It motivated me more. It sounded so much better and was more fun to play because of that. Plus, I made a big financial commitment and wanted to get my money's worth. (Cyndi wanted me to get our money's worth, too.) Either approach works. It just depends on your personality type and your budget. And of course let's not forget the third approach. That's: Pick-a-skill-that-doesn't-require-buying-stuff.

Whatever you need—whether you got it cheap, got it pricey or got it free—make sure it is accessible in your space. There's no need to make it harder on yourself to practice. Have your tools set up so that they're easy to get to when you're ready to rock. Then you can direct all your attention to the actual learning.

GET TO YOUR ZEN ZONE

Viktoria emphasized the importance of having a place where she could enjoy full concentration. She told me she needs privacy and peace—no distractions—in order to get to her place of focus. Acrobatics and aerial arts take 101% of your brain power. It takes your whole being, your entire essence. To be most effective in her practices, she needed to get to what I call the **Zen Zone.**

zen zone
/zen zohn/

noun
An incredibly focused and powerfully productive state of mind

BAMOLOGY DEFINITION

Getting to this ultra-productive mental state allows you to go deep in a limited amount of time. It lets you tap into that concentrated awesomeness that you're getting to be so good at. Your practice time is exponentially more potent because your mind is in the present moment, your energy is targeted on your goal, and you're not thinking about anything else.

Eliminating all distractions is key for getting to the Zen Zone. It's tough because we're bombarded with interruptions and beeping phones and people and hunger and meetings all the time. Like, right now, for instance, I'm totally distracted by the thought of peanut butter pretzels and a big tall glass of ice cold whole milk. (I can eliminate the distraction if I imagine it's 1% milk.) If we want to make the most of our time, though, we have to silence our phones, turn off the TV, close the browser window, put the "Do Not Disturb" sign on the door—do whatever it takes to clear the path to our focus. Make every single second count.

Sometimes I do all those things, I remove all the barriers, and I find that my own brain is the distraction. I'm in my own way. My to-do list is filling up valuable brain space or my anxiety about an upcoming event is zapping my clarity. This is another time when I find meditations and centering techniques particularly helpful.

While Cyndi and I were intensely discussing content for one of the book's chapters, we found ourselves crashing violently into a mental brick wall over and over again. My anxiety about finishing the book was growing like a weed in my mind. I was pacing the room, the volume of my voice growing by the minute, and sweat was starting to make its grand entrance through my palms. Cyndi stopped our conversation and said, "Bronkar, go outside for a few minutes. Do some breathing exercises." I resisted. She insisted. Rinse, repeat. Rinse, repeat. I finally gave in, took a break and did a quick session of breathing and head clearing—my **Two-Minute Tune-Up**. When I came back in, I felt like a new person. The issue we couldn't solve before suddenly had a solution. It's amazing what leaving the room and doing a little breathing can do for your perspective.

Getting rid of the roadblocks, outside and inside of yourself, will do wonders for your practice time. When you access your Zen Zone (cue the ambient synth sounds and contemplative flutes), you will make more progress, have more patience, and, quite frankly, have more fun.

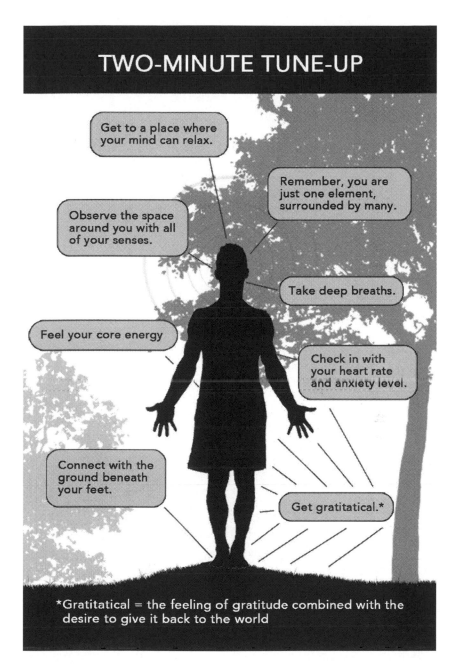

"The most difficult thing is the decision to act; the rest is merely tenacity."

– Amelia Earhart

CHAPTER 5:

GET UP AND GO

We've reached the step where the real *doing* happens. This is the action piece, the practice, the training. It's where we get to the meat and potatoes of it all. So let's go a little deeper. You and I both know it's not that easy. It's simple, but certainly not easy. This is where a lot of us run into resistance from our own selves. We're overwhelmed by all the other stuff we have to do in our daily lives. We feel frustrated when we don't make progress as fast as we hoped, or we just overthink it and never get started. We get off to a running start, but then fall short with the follow-through. Instead of Get Up and Go, we do the total opposite: Shut Down and Stop.

In addition, we sometimes run into resistance from the people around us. It's a real blow to the soul when we work so hard to break through barriers, and the people we love are intimidated by the true change taking place. They like the old you. They don't want to be left behind. Transformations are scary for everyone. Clinging to the normal, the usual, the familiar is our way of coping. But it's not how we grow.

There may be a lot of reasons to give up, but there are even greater reasons to keep going. Remember those intentions you set at the beginning of this journey, those pure motivations you discovered for yourself? Bring those back to the surface, hold those in the forefront of your mind, and visualize them coming to light. Do it now. Sit with that feeling. Keep your focus there. Your capabilities are boundless and real.

This chapter is a toolbox full of action steps to navigate you across oceans, over mountains, and through forests. If learning is a journey, there are bound to be flat tires, dead ends, and good ol' natural disasters. Consider this chapter to be the roadside service, the GPS, the knowledgeable tour guide—there so you can get out of the ditch and back on your way. Here are the four action steps:

1. Cheat the clock.
2. Design your time.
3. Break the loop.
4. Get in the groove.

CHEAT THE CLOCK

I get it. There's a severe time shortage going on. A deficiency of hours. A drought of minutes. A dehydration of seconds. Our world makes us feel as though we never have enough, no matter what we do. But guess what? We *all* have the exact same amount of minutes in our day. We just have to figure out how to cheat the clock and uncover some of those long-hidden minutes.

Our beliefs about the lack of space in our lives is a lot like my bedroom closet. I open the door, and I'm overwhelmed by the amount of clothes. There's nowhere I could possibly fit anything else, and I can never seem to find the shirt I want to wear, even though I know it's there. When I put away clean clothes, I tend to just close my eyes, dump the basket in, and run away because I don't want to deal with it. Cyndi comes along, helps me take everything out, organize it, create a place for each item to live, and all of a sudden, it's like I have ten times more closet space than I had before. Yet it's the same amount of stuff! I was using the space in a remarkably inefficient way.

It's possible that you, too, are suffering from an inefficient use of time, so I suggest you do some spring cleaning in your life. And actually, I would propose that you do it both literally and metaphorically. On the literal side, I get so much more done in a clutter-free office, it's ridiculous. All of a sudden my brain has more bandwidth to devote to creativity. I'm not looking for that missing saxophone reed or wondering what happened to the notes I took from my last rehearsal as I stare into a wasteland of notebook paper wreckage. There are some who argue that creative minds always have messy desks, and if that's you, more power to you. But if you do suffer from overwhelm, **try reducing the clutter** and see what happens.

Then have a look at your schedule. Where does your time actually go? A valuable exercise is to **keep a time log** for one week and write down what you do, when you do it, and for how long. Put it in that journal you started at the beginning of the book. And if you haven't started yet, I invite you to start now. You may come to realize that you're checking your Facebook status every 30 minutes for just 5 minutes at a time during your 16 hours awake. It seems like a small amount, no big deal—but do you realize that adds up to 160 minutes, which is over 2-1/2 hours of your day?! Two-and-a-half-hours of rolling your eyes at political posts, chuckling at kittens hugging baby chicks, and wondering how you got tagged again in a Ray-ban ad. Just as you are what you eat, you also are what you digitally consume. And maybe you are a master at time management. If you are, I salute you. But it's worth investigating.

Sometimes you just have to **multipurpose the time you do have**. One of my coaching clients, Steve, wanted to improve his guitar playing. Steve has a wife, two kids, and a full-time job, so he's got a busy schedule. Setting aside an hour to practice a few days a week was what he wanted, but he just wasn't meeting his goal. When he was at the brink of packing it in, he unearthed a gem of a realization. He was taking his son to baseball practice three days a week. For an hour, he would sit in the stands and skim the news, check and recheck his weather app, do a crossword—nothing particularly important. It was necessary to be there, for his son, so it wasn't wasted time, but he realized that he could use the time for more than one purpose. He started taking his guitar with him. He'd sit in the truck (because that's where

Could I listen to an audiobook
or have a call with my Coach
on the drive?

HOW LONG

TIME	ACTIVITY	
5:10pm	Drive home from office	30 min
5:40pm	Greet family + chat about day	20 min
6:00pm	Check Facebook / internet	20 min ← Combine/
6:20pm	Walk dogs	* 20 min cut back
6:40pm	Dinner with family	30 min internet?
7:10pm	Check Facebook / email + take out trash	15 min
7:25pm	Fix broken door handle	20 min.
7:45pm	Phone call with sister	* 10 min.
7:55pm	Watch Netflix	2 hr
9:55pm	Check Facebook + email	15 min
10:10pm	Chat with spouse	20 min.
10:30pm	Read book	20 min
10:50pm	Go to sleep	

Can I cut back
on TV?

* Could I have my phone
call while I walk the dogs?

he felt comfortable,) and do his hour-long rehearsal while he waited. He didn't have to cut out anything important from his day, and later he figured out his son was actually relieved that dad wasn't watching his every move. (His kid was in learning mode, too!)

Do you have chunks of time in your life that can be versatile like Steve's? Time that you can condense, time that you can use for more than one function, or time that you are doing some task that you don't even need to be doing in the first place? If you answered no right away, I'd ask you to take a closer look. Sometimes the moments are hidden and they're hard to see. It took Steve a while to see it, too. The truth is, none of us have an empty hour every day where we are sitting on a couch, thumb-twiddling, wishing that we had something to fill the time with. Get resourceful, clear the clutter, consider multipurposing. Make it happen.

DESIGN YOUR TIME

You carved out the extra time; now what are you going to do with it? It goes without saying that it's valuable stuff. Going in without a clear intention is a recipe for disastrous unproductivity. You might get results very similar to the results Cyndi gets when she goes to Target without a list of the exact things she needs. She comes home two days later with a dozen new frying pans, six vanilla scented candles and the entire Baby Department. And all she really needed was to get a birthday card for her mom.

Whether you've got 20 minutes or 3 hours—you need a system, a format, some sort of architecture for your efforts. You want the right plan of attack so you create maximum potency. *Concentrated awesomeness, people!!* Squeeze out every drop of your effectiveness by creating focus and intention when you go into practice mode.

Creating your structure is about looking at your starting point and then at your end goal and figuring out how to bridge the two together most efficiently. With saxophone, I intended to create a feel-good, high-energy piece for my one-man show. I did not intend to join an orchestra and be able to read sheet music on the spot. Therefore, my practices didn't focus heavily on reading and writing music. I focused on funk and blues progressions and learning scales so that I could improvise. Different intentions call for different approaches. Remember your goals when you are laying out the course.

"When you want to get good at something, how you spend your time practicing is far more important than the amount of time you spend."

—JOSHUA FOER, *MOONWALKING WITH EINSTEIN: THE ART AND SCIENCE OF REMEMBERING EVERYTHING*

There's never just one way to practice a skill, and the same method doesn't work for everybody. Try different options. Your practice for learning to cook is going to be different from my practice of learning to play the saxophone, which will be different from Joe-Bob's practice for learning to carve garden gnomes out of wood. If you want a *specific* plan for your *specific* skill, and you're having a hard time figuring it out on your own, remember this is what coaches and instructors are for. Use your crew! When I work one-on-one with clients, we focus on their individual needs and create a style molded to their preferences and with their end goals in mind.

There are a few general practice styles that have worked well for me and for the people I coach. I encourage you to try a combination of styles for the most powerful results. Alternate day-to-day or week-to-week, whatever works for you. You'll get variety, avoid boredom and make faster progress. Here are some styles to try out:

Keep It Fresh: This style is all about keeping your practice well-rounded and incorporating a nice variety of skills. If you get bored easily, this might be a good option to try. Break up whatever time you have into separate chunks and focus on a different aspect of the skill in each chunk. Make sure at least one of the sections focuses on a new challenge and another of the sections (preferably the last) focuses on something you enjoy and will easily achieve.

Drill It: Focus on one single skill for a whole session. This is all about honing in and fine tuning. For example, you are learning to speak Portuguese and you're having a tough time conjugating verbs. So you spend the entire hour-long session studying conjugations. Or you're working on giving presentations, but it's been brought to your attention that your enunciation is terrible. So you spend your whole session doing mouth exercises in the

mirror. I use this practice style often to overcome a weakness, isolating the problem and doing it over and over again until it's no longer an obstacle.

Buddy Up: I had an enlightening conversation with one of my juggling mentors, David Nayer (also an entrepreneur, mathematics expert, and poet, among other things). He talked about how collaboration is the perfect tool for increasing your perspective. You give your own; you get someone else's. Competition doesn't make sense in this model. Instead it's an opportunity to work together to create something even better than you could create individually. This style is about joining up with one or more of your peers and helping each other learn—sharing knowledge and building it together.

Soak it Up: In this option, you absorb knowledge from

someone else—whether it's by watching a video, reading a book or seeing it demonstrated live—and then you act on that new knowledge, practicing what you've learned. This is an opportunity to study other people's techniques, benefit from their mistakes, and get another perspective on your skill.

Get Schooled: This one's simple. Take a class, have a formal lesson one-on-one with an instructor, or work with a coach. Get feedback and critique from a pro. They are going to see things you don't and help you learn from mistakes in ways you can't on your own. This is why I always do Yoga in a class setting with a teacher. Downward Dogs are tricky, and

I can't leave my body to see my whole form accurately. A teacher can illuminate the fact that my arms aren't as straight as they should be, my feet are too close together... but hey, my head is in the right position!

Leave the Womb: There's nothing like real-world practice to kick your skill up a notch. But you have to step out of that safe, secure Womb of Creativity to do it. Practice in front of your family, your coworkers, your friends; or offer up your skill for free for someone in need. If you're learning an instrument, go play it on a public park bench. If you're learning how to design websites, offer to design one for free for a friend. If you're learning to paint, offer to do a mural at your kid's preschool. The idea is you share your skill in a public way that's low pressure.

Out of Body Experience: This style is great for any type of performance skill or any skill where you are publicly presenting something, whether it's a speech, a foreign language, dance, music, or theater. Acrobat and variety performer (and one of my  best friends) Simon Chabon would use this technique to film himself doing his back flips, stunts, and crazy gymnastic moves during his rehearsals. He would analyze it from an outside perspective and make adjustments to his form based on what he saw. You can also choose to record audio only, if that applies to your skill. Whenever I use this approach, Cyndi thinks I'm nuts because I refer to myself in the third person. "He really talks too much in that section. What is that guy doing?!" But it's helpful to detach so you can really see the opportunities for improvement and for praise.

 **Freestyle:** If I had specific instructions for this style, it wouldn't be freestyle. Do what you want, how you want, as much as you want, for as long as you want.

∽

Take a few minutes to think about what kind of structure would work best for you, your skill, and the time you have available. Pick a couple options from the list above, and make your plan. Write it down. Be specific about what you're going to achieve before you start your practice session. Plan it out into time chunks if you are working on more than one thing (e.g. 10 minutes of warm-up, 5 minutes of review from yesterday's session, 15 minutes of basic technique drills, 10 minutes of attacking a new challenge, 5 minutes of play). **Use a stopwatch or timer to keep you on track.** This has been a game changer for my personal productivity level! (Most smartphones have one included or have apps for purchase.) Put your practice sessions on your calendar so you can see the commitment. It is not a real priority unless it has a specific time and location attached to it. And don't forget to have fun!

BREAK THE LOOP

I was working on a new juggling skill—a seven ball force bounce juggle. That means I'm bouncing seven balls in a specific pattern onto a smooth surface while standing up on a ladder. It takes an insane amount of precision, impeccable timing and rhythm, advanced eye-hand coordination, and a little bit of crazy. Every ounce of my brain power is delegated to the task, and I must be completely 101% in the present moment.

So there I was, in the zone, doing the juggling pattern,

and things would be going great until the thirty-second mark. At this point, my pattern would fall apart and my focus would shatter into pieces. Seven round bouncy-ball-shaped pieces, to be exact. One ball would crash into another, exploding outward, causing a disastrous ripple effect on the other five balls. At 360 bounces per minute, that makes for an intense collision.

I was doing the same thing repeatedly, expecting a different result. And I was **OVER IT**. I was at my wit's end with frustration. As much as I had adopted the perspective that failure is learning, I was reaching my threshold. My failures didn't feel like positive opportunities to take flight anymore; they felt like sinking ships.

Frustration is normal, and it's inevitable. We *all* feel it at one point or another. The most talented, virtuosic, wonder-person you can imagine is not exempt from experiencing the head-pounding-against-a-brick-wall feeling. We feel this way when we make a mistake or we can't get over the hump of some challenge we're trying to conquer. The mistake plays in our head on a loop, over and over again. Our world becomes teeny-tiny because we're focused on the problem with microscopic intensity. We feel defeated, discouraged, trapped, upset, and sometimes totally useless. How do we get out of the cycle of UGH?

There are a couple of options. When I got stuck in my juggling practice, I decided I needed to **get another perspective**. I called up my juggling coach, David Nayer. When I told him about my struggles, he said, "You're holding your breath." Mind. Blown. I had never even factored that into the equation. The actual process of moving the balls was all I was focused on.

So the next day, I was ready to breathe. I warmed up and got going on the seven ball pattern, but my old routine took over and I forgot about my breath. (Silly me!) I was focused on my hands again. Right before ultimate ball destruction was about to happen, I remembered to inhale. Just in time! David was right. (Yay for coaches and mentors!) That simple shift in perspective changed everything. As soon as I incorporated breath into the juggling rhythm, I broke through and was able to make it over that hump. I never would have done so without getting that outside view.

"It's hard to read the label from the inside of the bottle."

—UNKNOWN

And the juggling story connects to my next point: **Breathe**. Breath has power! In moments of madness, I stop, close my eyes, and take deep breaths. My emotions are reset. I feel anchored, calm, and grounded in the present moment. The cool thing is that you don't have to wait until you're overwhelmed and defeated to breathe. Take deep breaths *before* you start working on something difficult or even at regular intervals during practice (or anytime!) Breathe in the inspiration, patience, and calmness. Breathe out concentrated awesomeness.

Sometimes you just need to **change the scenery**. Step away from it. Get out of the space for a few minutes. Disrupt the loop that's been playing in your head. And if you've got a set amount of time for practice and you can't afford to walk away, then just work on something else. **Move on**. Don't stay stuck. Go to the next thing on your agenda or work on something that's easy for you to achieve—or fun. A lot of times you'll come back to the challenge the next day and see that you've actually made progress.

GET IN THE GROOVE

Consistency in your practice is *absolutely paramount*. It must become a habit—something on your mind and in your body on a regular basis. All the steps of the process are connected, so think back to your motivations and intentions. Is learning a priority for you? Can you commit to building a habit so that you spend time every day on your skill? Even if it's just two minutes? This will truly make or break you, in terms of your learning success. If you don't have the opportunity to physically DO, then at least put thought into it. Put energy toward it. Meditate or visualize.

Cyndi is an avid exerciser and health nut (an almond, if I had to pick), and she loves to get her sweat on, but it wasn't always that way. When she started out, she had a thirty-minute workout DVD, and she would commit to doing ten minutes. Just ten. That's all she had to do. It was so easy to fit into her schedule. And some days that ten minutes was all she did. But on a lot of other days, she would finish her ten minutes and decide that twenty more minutes wasn't really that big a deal. The hardest part was just making the decision to do it, and then actually getting up and putting on her running shoes. Once she started the forward momentum, it was easier to keep moving in that direction. Over time not only did it become a habit, but she grew to really love it. In fact, it became a necessity for her. It was fun. She craved it. She became so connected to that habit that if she didn't get her workout fix every day, she didn't feel like herself.

Cyndi, 9 months pregnant, in Tree pose - November 2015

Our habits define us. They literally shape us as human beings. These behaviors that we do over and over again become imprinted in our brains and bodies. Doing something repeatedly becomes a part of you, and then it becomes easier to do on automatic. Here are a few tips for turning a behavior into a habit:

- **Create small, specific goals.** (e.g. "I'm going to practice for fifteen minutes, four days a week, for two weeks.")
- **Don't underestimate the importance of fun.** It's easier to commit to doing something if you look forward to it.
- **Change it up.** Boredom = Higher chance of quitting. Alternate the kinds of practice you do, and make sure there's variety.
- **Create conversations about your process regular-**

ly. Make sure you're checking in with your crew and updating them on both your struggles and successes.

- **Attach it to something else you already do.** Multipurpose, remember?! Listen to an audiobook about your skill on your commute to work. Practice your speech during your morning shower.
- **Reward yourself.** Celebrate your successes, even the tiny ones—whether it's by indulging in a banana split, announcing your wins on Facebook, talking your husband into giving you a foot rub if you meet your goals, or even just acknowledging it out loud. Be proud of yourself for making the choice to go after what you want.

Doing anything is better than doing nothing. It's all about shifting your mental norms. You're training your brain to get used to doing the thing you want to be doing. And if you want to be doing it, you're already going in the right direction.

"I think the most productive thing to do during times of change is to be your best self, not the best version of someone else."
– Seth Godin

CHAPTER 6:

SHOW UP AND ROCK IT

It was day 63 of my saxophone learning journey. The Disney Fantasy cruise ship I was on was sailing across the Caribbean seas toward white sandy beaches and tourist-ready merchants. I sat on the top deck of the ship, the fierceness of the wind jolting my body with rugged ocean vitality. Little girls in princess attire and little boys with Mickey Mouse bandanas tied haphazardly around their heads ran by, emitting high-pitched squeals and waving their arms hysterically. Let it be known that there is no shortage of sugar on cruise ships.

I was on the ship for work, performing my one-man show for thousands of happy vacationers, and tonight was the night I would debut my saxophone playing to an audience for the first time. On the inside I was like the hysterical princess kids, charged and wired. I had put hundreds of hours and all of my life force into this instrument, and I knew I was prepared to share it with the world. I was also nervous and anxious. Fear nipped at me like invisible mosquitos, hungry for my jittery blood. I took deep breaths and proclaimed: "I AM A SAX PLAYER!"

I had put so much of myself into this learning process, into this instrument, that to finally share it put me in a truly vulnerable place. I thought about it all day, and when the moment arrived, all the emotions were right there on the surface, pulsing in my chest. They seeped out in the form of sweat, but my mouth remained dry. I decided to open up to my audience in an attempt to gain support from them. I announced into the microphone: "I'm debuting a new skill tonight. I've never played the saxophone on stage in front of a live audience, but I want to do it for you guys tonight. Do I have your permission to give it a go?"

The audience was right there with me. They sensed my nervousness. They knew I was taking an emotional risk, but they were enthusiastic, responsive, and generous with their cheering. My performance was not perfect, by any means, but I was so in the moment that I didn't really care. Nor did they. I was having fun. They were having fun. I felt my goal of connecting with people manifesting. Something pure and magical happened. And it wasn't just because it was a Disney ship!

The performance ended. The theater emptied. The moms and dads steered the worn-out kids back to their rooms to sleep—drained from the sun, the nonstop activities, and the Mouse-shaped confections. I put away my show gear, changed clothes, and went back to the top deck. This time it was quiet, the night sky draped overhead like a warm quilt. The daytime adventure buzz settled into a nighttime restorative hum. I laid back on a sunbathing chair, looking up at the stars, and I put on my headphones, listening to one of my favorite Maceo Parker tracks, "Shake Everything You Got." I heard it with new ears. I was officially a saxophone player, and I felt validated by Maceo himself right then and there.

Showing up and rocking it happens when your skill finally becomes a natural, outward expression of you. You're using the skill in real-world application. In a way, you let go of it being *just yours*, and it becomes a force out there in the world. You've stepped out of your safe space and you are sharing it with others, no longer in practice mode.

You show up and rock it after your intentions have been fulfilled, your deadlines met, your goals realized. You have become *You 2.0*, you've reached Jedi status, you've arrived at what was once just a visualization in your mind. This step in the process isn't one specific moment or a particular thing you do, but rather how you live your life as a result of everything else you've learned along the way.

"Showing up and rocking it" is a lifestyle. It's *how* you approach your day-to-day. It's *how* you interact with others. It's *how* you respond to challenges. It's looking at the world with wider eyes and taking it all in with a more confident stance. This is an ongoing step. It's a mindset shift you've created for yourself, one that reminds you that you're capable of being bold, decisive, and certain. You deserve to reap the benefits of your hard work and effort, and you are a valuable presence on the planet.

There are four things you need to remember once you've arrived at this step in order to be able to sustain this good thing you've got going. If you neglect any of these points, you may find yourself faltering. The four elements of Showing Up and Rocking It are:

1. Leave the Womb.
2. Summon your strongest self.
3. Recharge your batteries.
4. Be limitless.

LEAVE THE WOMB

Six months after I started my musical journey with the saxophone, my life was shaken up like a James Bond martini. I was leaving my padded Womb of Creativity behind as Cyndi and I moved across the country from Los Angeles to Atlanta while expecting our first child. Nothing gives you more of a reality check than finding out you are about to become someone's parent. (You mean, they let you get pregnant *without* taking a year-long course and signing extensive documents??!!) Okay, we planned it, but still. Moving all your things and your life from one coast to another is no picnic. And as far as my learning was concerned, I was nervous because I felt dependent on the safe space that I had created in order to practice my instrument. This transition was a tough one.

One afternoon, just days from our L.A. departure, I stood in the man cave, staring into my Womb of Creativity. It was time to disassemble my safe and secure rehearsal haven. I carefully detached the padding from the walls and packed away the blankets. I'll admit I was a little sad. But soon we were on the road, our trusty tan mini-van filled to the brim with our valuables (including the saxophone, of course.)

The Grand Canyon welcomed us with a picture-perfect vista, and Williams, Arizona called upon us to "meet the Flintstones" at the Flintstones Bedrock City Park, where we posed for photos with Fred and Wilma and left with the theme song stuck in our heads. We took a detour to drive the Musical Highway in New Mexico a short stretch of road on Route 66 that plays "America the Beautiful" as your tires hit the ridges, but only if you are proceeding at 45 mph. A full double rainbow materialized during our rainstorm drive through Texas, stretching itself across opposite ends of the horizon in an otherworldly fashion—a moment for which no words could do justice. And then justice itself (in the form of a bored narcotics officer) mistook us for drug traffickers in Oklahoma. (What a disappointment that the only drugs to be found were 2 Advil circa 2003 stranded in the bottom of Cyndi's purse.)

But it was in Arkansas where the most monumental part of our cross-country extravaganza took place. We had already been on the road for 7 hours on the 5th day when traffic went from a glide to a trot to a crawl in a matter of minutes. Like a tired turtle, we ended up motionless on Interstate 40, among thousands of others. Travellers were soon turning off their engines, exiting their cars to stretch their legs, and we were informed there was a wreck a few miles ahead that wouldn't be clearing anytime soon.

As Cyndi and I sat there, Paul Simon's *Graceland* playing through the van's single working speaker, I had the overwhelming desire to play my saxophone. I said this out loud to Cyndi, almost like a question. But really I was asking myself. *Could I walk into the middle of the road right here, right now, with my saxophone and just start playing? Could I be totally fearless? Is this crazy?*

Cyndi gave me a half-smile and shrug. The of-course-you-are-going-to-play-the-saxophone-right-now look that Cyndi is so very good at. I wasn't *totally* fearless at all, but I decided to embrace my jitters. I grabbed the case, removed my sax, and walked into the road, right in the midst of an army of eighteen-wheelers. Something miraculous happened. The saxophone nearly played itself. In the middle of the most random highway scene, I found a way into my Zen Zone. I expected to feel vulnerable, like in the dreams people have where they show up to school in only their underwear. But I wasn't nervous. In fact, I could feel a sliver of confidence shining through. I was playing my instrument without concern at all for who might be listening. And the people all around us *were* listening! They went from being anxious and annoyed about the traffic jam to dancing to the music and laughing at this wacky character playing his instrument on the freeway! My Womb of Creativity was no longer the bathroom in the Los Angeles man cave, 1700 miles away. It was **within me**.

I made it through the beginning stages of learning the basics. I had my share of uncomfortable, clumsy, fumbling practice sessions, and now I could see definite improvement. Reaching this point doesn't mean we no longer fail or make mistakes. On the contrary, we may fail more spectacularly. And that's perfectly fine. We've come to understand that failing is learning. That falling means the opportunity to stand up again, taller. That making a mistake is the opportunity to scrape some more knowledge onto our plate.

When you've found your space, given yourself the tools, and put in the time and energy inside of that zen zone, your confidence will grow and you'll realize you don't need the training wheels anymore. (You may want to hang on to the handlebar streamers and bell, but that's just for style.) Your abilities increase and you start to move towards that *inner circle* of knowledge. The feeling of safety, of being in that cozy, padded womb is something that has built within you. It has transformed into an inner armor so that failing out there in front of others isn't so scary anymore. Or maybe it is scary, but we've become more brave. We pulse with courage instead of apprehension. **Being daring becomes our norm.**

SUMMON YOUR STRONGEST SELF

Hmmm... Summoning your strongest self? Bronkar, does this mean I should be turning into the Incredible Hulk? Or do I need a Harry Potter wand? Or should I be chanting something in a dark room around a crystal ball? You can do all of those things if you wish, but I'm talking about being the most confident, powerful, and boldly capable version of you. When I imagine my strongest self, I'm standing on top of a mountain, legs firmly planted like roots of a tree, arms stretching up and out. My head is tilted back and I'm looking up at the sky, acknowledging the warm sun on my face and the cool breeze tickling my skin. I climbed this mountain. I feel my heart beating, my lungs filling with air and then releasing, my blood flowing. It feels really good.

I encourage you to think about who your strongest self

is. If you want to summon it, you have to be able to recognize it. What does this version of you look like? Be this person in your mind. How do you carry yourself? How does it feel to be you—physically and emotionally? What do you say and do? Visualize this fearless, resilient, awesome human so that you can embody that person when needed.

Approaching daily life as this new, improved you is not without its challenges. I'm not even sure that there *is* such a thing as fearlessness. It really all comes back down to having the right tools in your belt. People that seem like they're afraid of nothing have only perfected the art of fighting the fear. These people have go-to practices and routines that get them over the hump of uncertainty into the soothing valley of confidence. They've learned how to tap into the focused headspace of the Zen Zone. As you step out of your safe space and put yourself out there, it's totally expected to feel nervous and unsure. It's scary, especially the first few times you do it.

I had the honor of being invited to perform a halftime show for a New York Knicks basketball game at Madison Square Garden. It was the middle of January, and the high temperature was 16 degrees Fahrenheit. (i.e. ABSURDLY cold.) On game day, Cyndi and I arrived early at the Garden to soundcheck and discuss the details of the performance with the production crew. The empty arena was massive and pulsing with a quiet heartbeat, a warmup to the deafening roar of the crowd to come. Nearly 20,000 empty seats faced me with expectation. There was a frenzy of feeling building inside of me. It continued to grow throughout the soundcheck and rehearsal, during the pre-game dinner, and as we waited backstage in our green room.

The hallway outside of our room was lined with posters of Billy Joel, Michael Jackson, and David Bowie (among others), from their performances at the Garden—a wall of legends who had been backstage in this very room, waiting to go on stage just as I was now. It was more intimidating than exciting. The game had started, and I could hear the wave of cheering and feel the intensity from the giant mass of people just a few feet away. All of a sudden, the frenzy that had been building all day exploded into a moment of uncontrollable self-doubt. *How am I supposed to entertain this enormous crowd?? I'm just one person, and I'm supposed to captivate 20,000 Knicks fans in the middle of a heated game? What am I doing here? I'm not ready for this. I'm not good enough. What do I have to offer?*

Even though I had lots of experience performing live shows, this felt like the first one. I was a sweaty-palmed, heart-galloping wreck. I told Cyndi that I was **so** ready for this moment to be over. She put down her giant pretzel, and when Cyndi puts down a giant pretzel, I know she's about to get serious. She said, "Are you kidding?? You've worked your whole career for this very moment. This is **THE MOMENT** you've been waiting for. You should be fired up and excited to get out there and show them what you've got!"

Something shifted in me when I heard her words. She was right (as usual). I had let my fears and insecurities swallow me whole. I lost sight of the moment and had neglected to perform the **personal ritual** that gets me mentally prepared. I snapped out of the self-pity, switched gears, and started my routine by counting to ten in a rhythmic fashion: 1-2-3, 2-3-4, 3-4-5, 4-5-6, etc. Reciting the numbers in a specific pattern targets my attention to the moment and jump starts my focus. Next, I closed my eyes and took a few deep breaths to cross over to the Zen Zone. Deep breathing lowers my heart rate, extinguishes anxiety, and aligns my body to my mind. I opened my eyes present, harmonious, and serene. From there, I moved into the final phase of my personal ritual—the warm-up. This consists of push-ups, sit-ups, squats, and stretches that get my physical body heated and ready to move.

Once my personal ritual was complete, I recited the **positive affirmation** I created for myself: "I am enough." These three simple words remind me that I am equipped with the tools that I need. It allows me to remember that I'm actually quite insignificant in the scope of the universe, and that often we make life much more complicated than it needs to be. It lets me simplify the thoughts and worries in my head to make room for a more positive flow. Once the words were spoken, I was newly inspired and ignited.

I entered the arena and welcomed the moment with open arms. I was still a tiny insignificant human being facing 20,000 screaming sports fans, but I was able to be my best and strongest self. And it was because post-pretzel Cyndi nudged me to find my Zen Zone and get prepared.

Rituals and affirmations can transport you to a place of extreme focus when you don't know how else to get there—whether it's a big moment of showcasing your skill or whether it's at the start of every single day to set the tone for achievement and accomplishment. I do this with my morning Back to Basics meditation. It's a personal ritual that allows me to ground myself and remember to operate in a place of gratitude, no matter what the circumstances.

What kind of personal rituals and positive affirmations could you create to help get you into the right frame of mind to summon your strongest self? You could sit in complete silence and do breathing exercises. You could listen to 70s rock full-blast while playing air guitar. You could visualize the success in your mind, or do a crossword puzzle, or rub a crystal, or do yoga. It could be saying "I'm amazing," doing cartwheels, or singing the alphabet backwards. Figure out what it is that brings you to the present and gets you ready to rock.

RECHARGE YOUR BATTERIES

Constantly summoning the most amazing version of yourself can take a toll on your body and mind if you neglect downtime. What you do in between your moments of greatness is just as important as the moments themselves. As a young adult, I was an aspiring tennis player. I watched and studied the greats—Andre Agassi, John McEnroe, Roger Federer—and I noticed that what really distinguished them from each other was their behavior after each point. A lot is happening when the ball is not in play. The players would very quickly reflect on the previous play. They would take stock of their opponent's form and notice where they were weak. Based on that observation, they might revise their approach for the next point. Then they would do a quick reset by spinning their racket, bouncing the ball a certain number of times, or taking a few recalibration breaths. All this would happen lightning-fast, but it had a direct effect on what would happen when the match resumed.

You may need only seconds or minutes to recharge your own batteries. For instance, you have a stressful interaction with a coworker, so you walk outside and take a few deep breaths. The fresh air revitalizes you, and the change of scenery resets your brain to zero so you can return to your office with a clear head. Or you may need a whole day to recharge, so you visit a museum with your best friend or go to a park with your family. Maybe you curl up in bed with a book you've been dying to read or stay in your pajamas and have an Indiana Jones movie marathon. And of course there are times when you need several days, or a week, or 2 weeks to recharge.

Don't ignore these times when that voice in your head is telling you to rest. I've done this in the past, only to crash and burn. I've either gone so hard that I've gotten physically sick, or I've lost steam for a project because I went into a full-on sprint at the start and never took a break. Make time to relax, meditate, and enjoy life.

Like the tennis pros, reflect on what's working in your life and what's not. Is it time to change your approach and tactics? Is it time to learn another new skill? Do you need a new person on your support team? Does your practice structure need reorganizing? Do you just need to turn off from being that "pro" for a little bit? Listen to yourself with real attention to detail. Then do what you need to do to recharge and be ready to summon your strongest self again.

BE LIMITLESS

It's time to come full circle. Remember when you started this book, and we decided that learning should be limitless—no-holds-barred, wide-open, full-on, and continuous? Well, now it's time for YOU to be limitless. Learning shouldn't be a start/stop, one-time-only event. It's a lifestyle, a way of being, a culture. It's time to embody the philosophy.

You will never know everything, and I don't know about you, but that fascinates me to no end. There's always room to grow yourself, to refine what you already know, or to go beyond it. Think of what the *You 3.0, 4.0,* or *5.0* could be. Say yes to moments. Create your opportunities. Don't sit around waiting for them.

Cyndi and I were driving up the I-5 from Los Angeles to San Francisco, and I had been playing saxophone for about three months. I was obsessed, playing it everywhere I went, for anyone who would listen. (Okay, I'll be real. I played it for people who *didn't* want to listen, too.)

On our 6-hour drive north, I practiced my scales in the passenger seat while Cyndi drove. [Read next sentence with highly sarcastic voice.] She *loved* being in a small, confined space without the capability to go anywhere else, listening to me run the same scales on repeat. [End sarcasm.] We pulled over at a rest area to eat lunch at a picnic table, and I serenaded Cyndi with smooth jazz while she ate her turkey sandwich. [Resume sarcasm now.] The unnecessary attention drawn to us while she ate and I played for her was really exactly what she wanted. [End sarcasm.]

Later on our drive, we pulled off the Interstate for an impromptu fruit stand stop. A local farmer was selling his first-class California cherries, apricots, plums, and almonds. We stocked up on the goods and were headed back to the car when I suddenly had the uncontrollable urge to play my saxophone for the farmers at the stand. This earns another sigh from Cyndi. (Don't get me wrong, she's very supportive of all my ventures. But I tend to operate on overdrive when I'm working on a new skill so I can't really blame her.)

I told the farmers that I really appreciated them being out there with their produce and that I wanted to play a song for them as a way to say thank you. You could tell by the look on their faces that this wasn't something that happened often. Or ever. But they were amused and intrigued, and I rocked out "When the Saints Go Marching In" for them. The summer sun was our spotlight and the dusty desert ground our stage, and they laughed and danced to my spirited rendition, squeaky notes and all. Their harvest-heavy eyes were brighter than before and their smiles a lot bigger. Cyndi and I were energized and renewed, too, their amplified joy cycling back to us. We created something magical *together*, all of us, seeded from authentic happiness. The moment ended with hugs and high fives. Cyndi and I got in the car, back on the road towards the Golden Gate, our smiles remaining long after we left.

Once again I was realizing that my learning goals were being achieved, and I was responsible for making it happen.

There were no bounds. I was putting myself out there as the saxophone player I wanted to be, and the universe was responding. These moments and opportunities that we create for ourselves, they aren't always perfect. They don't always result in laughing and dancing. Sometimes they are awkward. Sometimes they are uncomfortable. But they are real. And they are alive. You're out there doing it and that's the amazing part. Make a lot of mistakes. Mess up and fall down and trip over your feet. Laugh and learn. And most importantly, show up. And rock it.

"You're off to Great places! Today is your day!
Your mountain is waiting! So.....get on your way!"
– Dr. Suess

THE END... OR IS IT JUST THE BEGINNING?

Whoa. I made it to the end of the book. *You* made it to the end of the book. I'm so impressed with us! Mental high fives for all! The writing process has indeed been a bold learning adventure for Cyndi and me, and the whole thing has really been one giant Rock-It moment. Getting to the end feels good. But endings are just beginnings in disguise. There's always more...

BAM is about learning a skill, yes, but I hope you let it be about a lot more than that. The benefits of creating our own opportunities, saying yes to moments, and summoning our strongest selves are limitless. Learning is about growth, expansion, rejuvenation, and enjoyment. It's about keeping our minds young, flexible, and relevant. It's about applying our most authentic selves to anything we wish.

I met my goals with the saxophone. It was immensely gratifying. Feeling those dreams actualized is a feeling like no other. And using my skill out in the world was and continues to be fulfilling. I've played in the park at night for homeless people; I've gotten out of my car and played in the middle of the freeway, while everyone was stuck in a traffic jam; I've played on the edge of the Grand canyon, notes bouncing rock to rock; I've played for bikers, babies and businessmen on sidewalks, shorelines and stages. The saxophone is just a tool I use to amplify my essence (the purest, most real part of me) to the world.

Bronkar on the edge of the Grand Canyon - June 2015

I'm no more special than anyone else. We all have this potential to create our own concentrated awesomeness. Sometimes it's hard and sometimes it's easy. But it's really, *truly* worth it. We are conductors of our own symphonies, engineers of our own master plans, and leaders of our own charges.

My system is just one in a world of many learning systems. I'm sharing it because it has worked for me, it has worked for people I've coached, and because I believe it can work for you. Oftentimes the main thing holding us back from going forward is ourselves. Sometimes we have to politely tap on our own shoulder and ask ourself to move out of the way. And if that doesn't work, we knock him down!

Give the process your full commitment. If you're not really into it, it **won't** work. If you don't care, no one else will either. It's an adventure! And it's **bold**! Have fun. Laugh. Play. Bring your A-game. As you move forward in your journey, don't forget that you can also go back. *"But that's crazy-talk, Bronkar! Why would I willingingly go backwards, other than to do the moonwalk?"* Because the process isn't linear; nor is it a one-way street. I don't know about you but I hate one-way streets. Especially when I'm trying to navigate a new city. It's so confusing and I usually end up getting lost, even with Siri's help. Actually, *especially* with Siri's help.

The process is fluid and flexible. We can add to our crew at any time. We can change our Womb of Creativity whenever we are ready to. We are constantly working on keeping the right mentality. We have a Rock-It moment, then we go back and practice some more.

I encourage you to share your story of learning as often as you can, with as many people as you can. Why? Because that's the reason we wrote this book. To stir up a storm of momentum in other people's ecospheres. The more people we have around us that are in growth mode, the easier it is to be in that mode ourselves.

Have you seen the BBC nature documentary Planet Earth? There's an episode about the ocean in which a school of millions of sardines are driven to the surface of the water by another predator fish, which attracts seabirds that dive down into the water to join the feed. Sharks and dolphins are attracted by the spectacle and join in, corralling the sardines into edible pockets, keeping them trapped at the top. And even a whale comes to take part in the feast. What's my point? The sardines of knowledge are right here! There's plenty for all of us. Let's create a learning frenzy that we can all benefit from.

Our world is buzzing with possibility. If you listen closely, you'll hear it, too. Cyndi and I composed a song for Elijah before he arrived with the lyrics, "Baby, baby, baby, get ready for the big world." We are born into what-ifs, maybes, and hopefullys (and a few definitelys). There are discoveries to be made, innovations to be imagined, and revolutions to be started. You are smart. You are strong. And you have the power to do great things. I know it. So put the book down and go DO.

potential
/puh-ten-shuh l/

noun
The thing you are bursting with

BAMOLOGY DEFINITION

COACHING

Are you interested in finding your own life coach or performance coach? Awesome! I'd love to help. If I don't have an opening or if I'm not the best fit for you, I can most likely help you find someone who is. Like if you want to learn to make origami out of poison ivy or learn to style hair with a blowtorch. Send me an email here: coaching@bamthebook. com with the Subject: "Interested in Coaching" and let me help you round up your crew!

BOOK EXTRAS

- Bold Achievement Manual (a workbook of action steps, questions and guidance to go with each chapter)
- Bonus videos
- Audio meditation tune-ups
- Resource lists
- Worksheets

Available for free at bamthebook.com/extras

ACKNOWLEDGEMENTS

We want to thank our amazing support team for keeping the content as *bamalicious* as it could be: Tracey Owens, Tricia Molloy, Dez Thornton, Evan "Witt" McGown, Natasha Kaluza, Jamie Coventry, Corey Perlman, and Tom Nixon. David Corbin, thank you for being the B.A. who led us in the right direction to discover our writing voice. Cheers to Aaron DeWayne Williams, Lance Ringnald, Viktoria Grimmy, Liz Shiflet, David Nayer, Chase Brantley and Bill Forchion for sharing your knowledge and experiences. Elijah, thank you for forcing us to make use of our own concentrated awesomeness in between your naps and feedings. Shout-outs to the incredible National Speaker's Association peeps, Trevor Crane and the BBB team, Hayley Foster, Gerry Bronkar, and Andy McIntyre (the juggler in the park). Bill Barr, we love you for keeping us on track with our truest selves. This book would not be the same without your influence and input. Brian and CeCe, we are grateful to you both for laying a solid foundation in us to focus, commit and follow through. Much love to Cheryl and John Lee for looking after our little Bobbin while we worked, and Dottie and Lamar for giving Tiny Lion Productions its first push. Love to Jenn for supporting us even amongst a big move to the west, Daniel for sharing your book-writing expertise, Megan and the Monday Morning Moms for saving Cyndi's sanity, and Dan Thurmon, the birth giver to "BAM"—a beacon of light shining brightly in this world. And finally, a massive thank you to Diana Kokoszka for believing in Bronkar and giving him the deadline to complete this book. Without you it may never have gotten finished.

Made in the USA
Columbia, SC
31 March 2019